T0365623

Brand Therapist

Using **Psychology** to transform the way
We create personal **brands**

by **Yamilca Rodriguez**

Brand Therapist
USING PSYCHOLOGY TO TRANSFORM THE WAY
WE CREATE PERSONAL BRANDS
Copyright © 2023 .

iUniverse books may be ordered through booksellers or by contacting:

iUniverse
1663 Liberty Drive
Bloomington, IN 47403
www.iuniverse.com
844-349-9409

Because of the dynamic nature of the Internet, any web addresses or links contained in this book may have changed since publication and may no longer be valid. The views expressed in this work are solely those of the author and do not necessarily reflect the views of the publisher, and the publisher hereby disclaims any responsibility for them.

Any people depicted in stock imagery provided by Getty Images are models, and such images are being used for illustrative purposes only. Certain stock imagery © Getty Images.

ISBN: 978-1-6632-4993-7 (sc)
ISBN: 978-1-6632-4994-4 (e)

Library of Congress Control Number: 2023901003

Print information available on the last page.

iUniverse rev. date: 10/22/2024

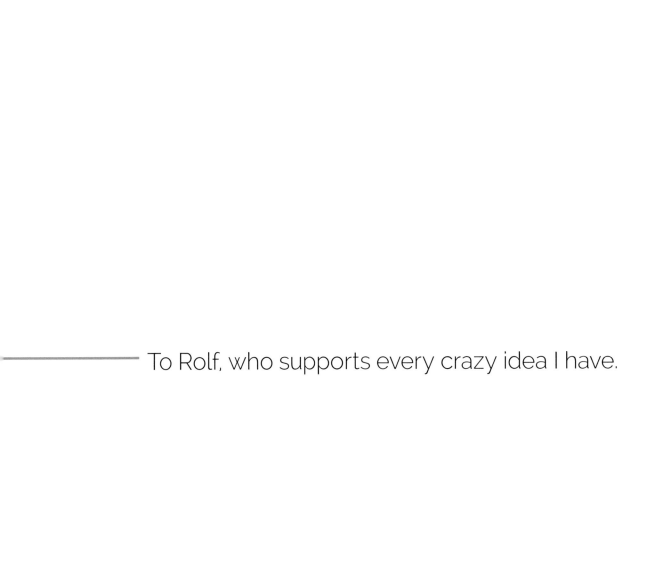 To Rolf, who supports every crazy idea I have.

Content

Part 1

Part 2

Part 3 ———

Foreword

"So, who are you?" I paused, and my face must have had a blank stare. *Excuse me? She knows who I am*. The question was asked again, "Who are you?" I answered with my title and the name of my company. "NO! Who are you?" At that moment, I realized I could not articulate who I was, and my response was ambiguous. *Oh, my! Does this suggest that I cannot define who I am as a person?* Thank goodness for Yamilca Rodriguez, aka the Brand Therapist.

Yamilca's book, *Brand Therapist*, shows you how to transform the way you create your personal brand. This book clearly outlines that if you don't have a personal brand, you will leave little or no impact on business and the world. Since that's not what I want, nor is it my purpose in life, I continued to read, understand, and implement. But to do this, you must do your homework. Get a journal and write down all the questions and your answers. Discuss this with your mentor, or do the homework with your accountability partner. Do the work in a peer advisory group; if you don't yet have one, find one. Find at least one of these resources today if you don't have any of these relationships. It's never too late!

As for me, I have personal mentors, advisors, and accountability partners. I also belong to and facilitate peer advisory groups for women who run businesses with six-figure gross revenues and those who run multimillion-dollar companies globally. I have worked with multicultural, multiethnic, multinational businesswomen for over 25 years, and I'm still learning and perfecting who I am. But after reading this book, I could apply the tools and techniques, along with my consultation with the author. I am ready! But be mindful that to understand archetypes, it's imperative that you read the book and answer all the questions and complete all the exercises. I did, so now I'm happy to share what I've learned.

As a former C-suite executive and entrepreneur, now serving as a consultant, here's some free advice: Take time to engage with *Brand Therapist*.

In my 40 years working in the business community, I've been engaged with many unique personalities. My education comes from the University of Michigan, with a major in psychology, plus different certifications in human resources, strategic management, and advanced group facilitation, which have enabled me to underscore the importance of assessing ambiguous personalities and relationships. I did not have the tools or techniques offered in this book, so I sometimes did not identify individuals properly or promptly. There were times when the result was disastrous.

There were times it was contentious because I did not understand the archetype. In needing to understand individual archetypes, I overlooked the impact this had on my social capital.

By harnessing my experience, I could identify five attributes of successful entrepreneurs and executives (courage, connection, collaboration, communication, and cultivation). Still, they became more enhanced once I understood the different archetypes and incorporated the techniques offered by *Brand Therapist*. Now I can work comfortably with individuals and know they are not adversaries, but allies. My "aha moment" has taught me how to scale in business by aligning my brand with my purpose, but understanding that the different archetypes change the narrative to an opportunity, not a threat.

The author explains, in detail, how and why your brand must align with your purpose. She speaks to how you must position your brand and business for success. If you know yourself, you will trust your instincts, and only then will you be able to identify the difference between you and another entrepreneur or company.

The most compelling part of the book for me was understanding who my superfan was. Once I understood who they were, I saw that their leadership style was about power. My superfan wants to revolutionize platforms and bring about new ways to think about "old" systems. They are pretty comfortable sharing their beliefs by breaking all the rules. They have a light and dark side, sometimes viewed as villains or bullies. They are bold-disruptive-unique! My superfan, the Outcast, is my opposite; they know they cannot do what I do. The author's book makes it very clear that tension breeds potential. The potential for me is to maintain focus and continue to create new ideas and opportunities for the women I serve.

This book has helped me identify my personal brand and my archetype. I now know who my fame character and superfan are. Since I can identify my personal brand, it is one that people will know about, trust, and follow.

Thank you, *Brand Therapist*! Thank you, superfan! You both are testimony to the fact that Women Elevating Women will capture hearts and souls.

Keep elevating, Brand Therapist!

Betty J. Hines
Women Elevator
Aka Founder & CEO of Women Elevating Women (W.E.W.)

Preface

Who looks outside, dreams; who looks inside, awakes.

—Carl Jung

The Art of Creating Fame

This Book Is for You...
If you want to be your best and understand that there are new rules of engagement to thrive in this new economy.
If you want to leave the mediocre and are willing to do what it takes to thrive—i.e., be on the runway to share your passion, story, idea, business idea, service, or product.
If you understand times have changed and that standing in the limelight is the fastest way to increase your bottom line.
If you are willing to take risks, stand on the runway, and share your gifts.

This Book Is Not for You...
If you believe that your achievements, products, or services will speak for themselves.
If you do not believe in the power of the person to make a difference.
If you do not believe that the power of being known for your craft can triple your bottom line.
If you do not believe in the power of authenticity to create credibility and, thus, expand your business.
If you believe storytelling should be relegated to children's books and fiction.
If you would rather rely on how things have always been done.

What Can You Expect?

In this book, you will learn about the concept of brand economy. You will see how personal branding is an honorable pursuit.

You will learn how to navigate this new world of personal branding.

You will learn why things have stalled and what to do to build your business, organization, or brand.

You will receive suggestions on finding your personal message and brand.

You will gain a guide to finding the essence of who you are so you can build your fame profile consistently.

You will learn about the power of tension and how it is a requirement for success.

You will gain clarity and comfortably develop a game plan that can be executed and advance you toward a meaningful and fulfilling life.

Your essence is your signature. Powerful branding opens a new world full of exciting opportunities. Branding is the fragrance that sets you apart from the pack.

Success can come as fast as you are ready to go. It's as simple as facing fear and knowing you will succeed.

Fame is for you when you are ready to muster the courage to live out your legacy in honor of yourself and future generations.

Why Did I Write This Book?

I wrote this book so more people could create their authentic selves. When we start a business, we spend so much time figuring everything out without seeing what's right in front of us. We need to go to the innermost layer of our soul.

I wanted people to go out into the business world, knowing that great brands have unlimited budgets and resources. I also noticed that people were scared to put themselves out there, hid behind the brand's name, and had no idea of their brilliance. They did not know that they were admired and that people were dying to learn more about them as real humans with hearts and souls.

I understood people wanted to impact the world but didn't know how. By reframing, I could reveal what they already knew about themselves and look at it from a different perspective.

I want business owners to have a deep connection with their audience and reveal their hearts and souls to them so the customer can feel cared for, loved, and listened to and so that we can all have a better experience in this unique world.

About The Author

Yamilca Rodriguez was born in Caracas, Venezuela. At the age of eight, she moved to San Diego, California, with her family. When she was fourteen, she moved back to Venezuela and lived in Cumana, a small town on the coast. A year later, her father got a job at the University of Macomb, Illinois, and a year after, the family moved back to Venezuela to a small town in the Andes Mountains. From a very young age, she has been a world traveler.

Yamilca has been a guest professor at Philadelphia University Strategic Design MBA.

She has a Master of Business Administration from Thomas More University and holds a Bachelor of Science in Industrial Design from the University of Cincinnati College of Design, Architecture, Art, and Planning (DAAP).

Yamilca is best known as a former brand leader at the most significant brand-building company globally, the Procter & Gamble Company. For decades, she has been helping brands and individuals create unforgettable experiences. She was featured in Forbes Magazine, The Voice-Tribune, The Courier-Journal, Today's Woman, and StyleBlueprint. She is a three-time #1 bestselling author of *Women Who Boss Up*, *Ignite Entrepreneur*, and *Women Gone Wild*.

She has worked on many billion-dollar brands like SKII, Olay, and Crest 3D White, to name a few. She is a TEDx speaker and has spoken nationally and internationally. She has been nominated for *Most Admired Women* in the beauty category for two years in a row. She has done everything, from teaching yoga to teaching MBA students design thinking.

When Yamilca isn't creating bespoke experiences, she travels the world, helping women grow their businesses fashionably. Outside work, she loves spending time with her husband and stepson in their Kentucky home.

INTRODUCTION:
THE POWER OF THE BRAND "YOU"

The brand is all about "you." The term *brand* comes from the Old Norse word, *brandr*, which means "to burn." Livestock was branded over 4,000 years ago. Branding went from farming to real estate, to artists and artisans claiming their work. Then to factories owning their products and companies claiming their products.[1] Over the centuries, the usage of the word *brand* has evolved to credit the inventors of products and services.

Instead of livestock branding, today it is about you. Social media is entirely about "you." You are your brand, and you are the product. To define your brand, you need to know who you are. People want to know who you are so they can connect with you. What are the characteristics that set you apart from your competition? What's the story that sets you apart from the rest of the people who do what you do? Your brand is unique, and only you can define its character.

Who Invented Modern Branding?
Modern branding started in the 50s with companies like P&G, and I saw this play out in real time while working at the same company. Brand management was developed by consumer goods companies like P&G, Unilever, and General Foods. Brand managers were responsible for ensuring their product had a brand character so it could differ from competitors' products.[2]

---

[1] Taylor Holland, "What Is Branding? A Brief History," Skyword, August 11, 2017, accessed January 11, 2023, https://www.skyword.com/contentstandard/branding-brief-history/.

[2] Marc de Swaan Arons, "How Brands Were Born: A Brief History of Modern Marketing," The Atlantic, October 3, 2011, accessed January 11, 2023, https://www.theatlantic.com/business/archive/2011/10/how-brands-were-born-a-brief-history-of-modern-marketing/246012.

Twenty years ago, brand characters were part of everyday products. Making sure they had a personality to connect to the customer. We were making them feel like the brand was a person so they could relate to the product. Today, people are brands whether they know it or not, and we need to connect to people through our stories and values.

What Is a Personal Brand?

A personal brand defines you as a person. Who are you? What are your values? What do you stand for? Defining your personal brand gives you leverage in the business world. Today, people want to talk to people, not products of companies, and people want to know people and what they are all about.

Why Have a Voice?

To become a personal brand is to use your gifts and find your unique voice. Using your voice is about doing something solid with your thoughts, ideas, and opinions. Your story is one that you are uniquely qualified to tell—there is no one else who can do it for you. Even if you had an identical twin who grew up beside you in the same house, with the same parents, rules, religious beliefs—everything—you would not have the same story to tell. Everything stems from a personal place; revealing it to the world means being vulnerable and exposing yourself.

The stories of others have always fascinated me. I like to spend hours reviewing other people's family photo albums and asking for stories. I believe in people's hope, magic, and potential. I am fascinated by the incredible beings I meet in the world. I want to hear their voices, those who share opinions with me and see things differently than I do. I want to listen to them, with all their unique biases and influences.

Our voices matter because they connect with others. They will find others who understand and will therefore foster community, friendship, and belonging.

Our voices matter because they expose our truth and show what it means to be us.
Our voices bring light to our corner of the world.
Our voices matter because they help to create change. By sharing our thoughts, we will all come one step closer to understanding each other, ourselves, and what it means to be

human. You have an enormous capacity for change regardless of your career, status, or ideology.

Your Brain, Your Brand

Personal branding is a conscious endeavor. Personal branding is all about the way we behave and our values. The only way to do personal branding is with intentionality, by bringing the unconscious to the conscious. Personal branding has a lot to do with psychology.

Let's look at what the collective unconscious means. The collective unconscious can be a complex term to understand. Carl Jung coined the word to represent the part of our brain that contains memories we are unaware of, originating in the inherited component of our brain. Think of it as a computer. The hard drive is where all the data you have collected from different sources and the ones you have created are stored.[3]

Yet, there is more. Jung proposed that our unconscious mind comes into the world containing history, thoughts, and behaviors that connect us all as humans. [4]

The two most influential psychologists of our time had two different viewpoints on our personal experience. Freud believed that our personal experience made us who we are, and Jung said personal experience exists to develop who we already are.[5]

The difference between Jung and Freud was that Jung believed we had a past beyond birth and were connected through our past lives and genealogy. Freud thought we came to this world with a blank slate, and our environment and experiences created our reality.

---

[3] "Collective Unconscious," Encyclopedia Britannica, n.d., accessed January 11, 2023, https://www.britannica.com/science/collective-unconscious.

[4] Sheri Jacobson, "The Collective Unconscious - What Is It, and Why Should You Care?," Harley Therapy™ Blog, May 11, 2017, accessed January 11, 2023, https://www.harleytherapy.co.uk/counselling/what-is-the-collective-unconscious.htm.

[5] Ibid.

How Does This Relate to Personal Branding?

Psychology: The scientific study of the mind and how it influences behavior.[6]

This is where the journey begins: at the level of psychology, human behavior, and, yes, archetypes. Archetypes are universal symbols and images stored in our memory bank. Therefore, I use archetypes in my personal branding methodology.

Jung believed we came into this world with a memory bank called the collective unconscious. This bank allows us to integrate an archetype, and we can choose to activate and uncover the layers of this unique archetype and bring it to the conscious level.

Using the unconscious mind to uncover the ultimate potential is the way to access our innermost gifts and use them for good. Your personal brand is your personal power. We all have it, and we all have access to it.

Your Brand Therapist will guide you through the ins and outs of navigating the fame universe.

Questions to Ask Your Unconscious Mind:
- – *Who am I?*
- – *What is my purpose in this lifetime?*
- – *What are my gifts?*
- – *What is my potential?*

---

[6] Oxford University Press, "Definition of 'psychology noun' from the Oxford Advanced Learner's Dictionary," Oxford Advanced Learner's Dictionary, 2019, accessed January 11, 2023, https://www.oxfordlearnersdictionaries.com/definition/english/psychology.

Chapter 1

From the Unconscious to the Conscious

Trust yourself. Let self-awareness be your science.
Let self-discovery be your research. Let your intuition be your expert.
Let your endless curiosity be your teacher. And, above all, find out
what makes you smile. That is the most important study you can ever
undertake.
—Vironika Tugaleva

I started writing this book a year ago. All the twists and turns guided me to where I am today. I want this book to teach people to understand their personal brand. In today's world, we are here to serve others and share our true selves. Authenticity comes from within.

Once we understand that, we can share ourselves without fear, judgment, hurt, or shame. Some of us go through life numb and show up as half of who we are. This has been revealed to me, and I have had to uncover layers and layers of the past that I was holding on to. You are only sometimes aware of what you project, but I have made it my goal to show up for my clients in a way that helps them express their true essence. Yes, I can make anyone's brand beautiful and fabulous, but I have learned that if my client is not ready for fame, they will not succeed.

My branding journey began in 2001, right after 9/11: October 1, 2001. That was when I started my career at the Procter & Gamble Company. I had graduated from the University of Cincinnati and made it to one of the best branding companies in the world. P&G was the best school for branding you could ever go to, and as a recent design graduate from DAAP in Cincinnati, I was living the dream.

I knew I didn't want to be one of those designers stuck at a desk day in and day out. I felt fortunate to start my design career as a Design Manager, which meant I managed brands, and I was more like a creative director overseeing the strategy and vision for where the brand was going.

I started my career in innovation, where I designed the future of brands. I created worlds for the company's brands and what they would look like in 2020. The great thing about starting at P&G when I did was that it wanted designers to have a seat at the table. Before 2001, designers were called Art Directors. There was a revolution taking place, and P&G was at the forefront. It was a super-exciting time to be there and watch how this transformation unfolded, almost like having a front seat at the movie theater.

We broke ground with revolutionary design ideas, like designers having a seat at the table, which was unheard of in the industry. We became part of a multifunctional team, we led projects on a grand scale, and we ran design thinking workshops so we could revolutionize the industry.

Designers were few and in demand, and we worked only on billion-dollar brands. During my eight years in innovation, I led projects worldwide, meeting our customers, and going home to understand human behavior. I met Sabrina in my second year at P&G. Although I hesitated working with a new team, it was the best thing that had ever happened to me. Sabrina was a wealth of knowledge and introduced me to archetypes.

Archetypes changed my life and the life of my teams. Once we knew what archetype we defined on a brand, we could move the project much faster, and the team couldn't believe the speed and accuracy of our design ideas. But it wasn't something Sabrina and I explained to the team; it was more what we did behind the scenes to achieve the business goal we had been entrusted with.

Sabrina and I would ask the team a few questions until we had enough information to work on our ideas. We conducted research to validate our concepts and then worked on the universal model to execute our ideas. It was genius. I made a name for myself as the go-to person for persona profiles. Everyone was impressed with how the interpretation of persona profiles helped everyone on the team to execute excellently.

I worked on super-exciting projects and had so much fun inventing new products, understanding deep consumer insights, and creating brand excellence with each project. This went on for eight years. Sabrina moved on, and I decided it was time for me to move from innovation to brand identity. I had done a few brand identity projects and loved our current business because it allowed me to see my project on the shelf in a couple of years, so I moved to brand identity full-time. I had transitioned to what I called the "dark side." The design world knew I had an eye for beauty and a creative mind to go with it. So, I became the brand identity leader for Oral Care.

Brand identity was different, but I thrived and loved working on the current business. I still used universal models and archetypes to drive brand coherence in consumer products.

After a while, I noticed it was time to leave the company and continue my life elsewhere. Yet I was still stuck in my former P&G life, and I had a hard time removing that identity from my new one. I decided to enter an entirely new world, "the fashion world," so I could understand through my own life that I could change my identity. My first attempt was at the unconscious level.

Two years later, I was called back to perusing the archetypes and fell into helping entrepreneurs understand their brands so they could build a business. I took the tools I had developed in the branding world and reconnected with Sabrina. Sabrina helped me see how I could use this new and evolved theory to help my clients. I worked on content and concepts and began creating the world of personal branding, starting with the foundation level, the fame essence, and taking entrepreneurs to a new and conscious brand level.

Questions to Ponder:
– *What is your brand essence?*
– *What are the core values of your brand?*
– *What is the impact you want to leave?*

Chapter 2

To Be, Or Not To Be

*When you are no longer able to change a situation, you are challenged
to change yourself. And that changes everything.*
—Viktor Frankl

There comes a moment when you can no longer accept things and circumstances the way they are and the way they have always been. After working in a corporation for over a decade, I started my entrepreneurial journey. I moved to a new city and was ready to work in a new company. I got a job as Director of Multicultural Marketing Services. Shortly after starting work for this agency, I realized it was not for me, but I stayed for a year. Those nine months of excruciating pain were enough to change my life. The employees did not want to change the way they were working. The clients were not communicating the right and relevant information. It was a very frustrating time for me. I met incredible people, and I was forced to do something new. I thought, *What if I start my own business? What if I could use all the skills I learned in corporate to help people brand themselves?*

The Pioneering Impact of Procter & Gamble on the Entertainment Economy
American multinational consumer goods corporation Procter & Gamble was one of the first companies to sponsor daytime serial dramas on the radio to advertise their products to housewives in the 1930s. The shows were associated with sponsors, such as P&G's cleaning products, and were dubbed "soap operas." If any company knew about the entertainment economy back then, it was P&G.

When I started working there, I was naïve about how decisions were made. It was all about advertising. Our bread and butter were the company's "untouchable" brands like Tide and Pampers. That meant we were not to make any significant changes in their marketing as long as the money was rolling in. But there was a point when Pampers suffered, and every change made felt like a huge risk. The change could be visual, like a new picture, a different font for the words on the package, or a color change. The design had many variables, and any change to any variable mattered, even if it was just moving words around.

When I started at P&G, I was in what they called the "paper" category, which meant Pampers, Always, Tampax, Bounty, and Charmin, and not "goop" like most P&G products that were liquids. Although I worked on Always, we met regularly with the other teams. I had arrived at a time when "Design" with a capital "D" was starting to take center stage. Alan G. Lafley was an outstanding CEO. He understood the importance of design and wanted Design to have a seat at the table in every category.

I remember that Pampers had gone through an overhaul, going from a performance-driven category to a purpose-driven one. Pampers was all about dryness and healthy skin, but consumers were more concerned about emotional drivers at this turning point, and Pampers was in dire straits. I had heard rumors that Procter & Gamble was going to sell Pampers. The savior of the diapers category was Jim Stengel. He pioneered a considerable cultural shift in how we looked at brands. With Pampers, he made a major push to focus on the bigger picture—helping moms—rather than wicking away moisture. Jim's book, *Grow: How Ideals Power Growth and Profit at the World's Greatest Companies*, talks about a branding ideal being the taking of Pampers from $3.4 billion in sales to $9 billion.

What came out of the entertainment economy was a collaborative approach to advertising. P&G was all over the world, but we had tended to work in silos. We then realized we had to do something to bring teams together—not just teams, but brands and our external partners.

The word *holistic* wasn't used as often then as it is now, but that was the approach we had to take. We looked at every possible channel and execution of the brand to take a decisive stand in the market. Multidisciplinary approaches began to trickle down in every team. Connecting the disciplines made us more powerful, and our partnerships with other agencies became more interconnected. Brand summits became frequent so we could learn from other disciplines, and our agencies became a global powerhouse of billion-dollar brands.

P&G had difficult years, but the brainpower in that company was incredible, and we always came out strong. I loved working in an environment where diversity of thought and innovative strategies were a must. Launching a product that was ahead of its time happened often. I worked on some exciting future-driven ideas that never even hit the market.

P&G spent $7.867 billion on advertising in the fiscal year 2013–14. That was $1.116 billion more, an additional 14 percent, than recorded in the previous fiscal year. That marked the beginning of the fame economy.

Fame economy had a slow start, just like most breakthroughs. Trends usually start way before they become something; sometimes, they become nothing. "At the end of 2012, they were 376 million of the 1,056 million total (or 35%); now they are 285 million of 1,230 million (23%). The shift has been coming for a long time: at the end of 2012, Facebook said that in December 2012, 'mobile daily active users exceeded web daily active users for the first time.' But it's taken a while for that to become embedded enough for mobile-only to overcome desktop-only."[7] I remember this because I worked at an agency in 2015, and we knew Hispanics were way above the percentage of mobile users.

Today, we are challenged to share more, entertain more, and be more visible. This is the new normal; for some of us, this is not fun. People working in companies, entrepreneurs, and anyone looking to do more and have an impact must put themselves out on the ethers.

The key is to showcase a personality that you are aware of and to be conscious of that identity. Everything is done seamlessly with intentionality, knowing and understanding your true essence.

Questions to Ponder:
- *What are the social media channels that work for you?*
- *How are you being transparent with your audience?*
- *What are the values you want to share with the world?*

---

[7] "Facebook's Mobile Journey Has Only Just Begun, but Already Makes Money," The Guardian, February 3, 2014, accessed January 11, 2023, https://www.theguardian.com/technology/2014/feb/03/facebook-mobile-desktop-pc-platforms.

Chapter 3

Avoiding the Call

There is no greater gift you can give or receive than to honor your calling.
It's why you were born. And how you become most truly alive.
—Oprah Winfrey

I kept avoiding the brand world. I became famous in the fashion world but couldn't see any future in it, so I decided to return to my love of branding.

I went into fashion because I wanted to be a fashion designer at one point in my life. When I looked at Carolina Herrera as a role model, I couldn't see myself in that world. During the last few years in my corporate job, I was looking for another career and tried a few different roles. The first one was as a yoga instructor. I studied yoga for three years. First, I did my yoga certification. Then I went on to study Ayurveda. I taught a few classes and did a few Ayurveda workshops, but I didn't feel it was going anywhere.

I decided to design a line of skirts. I created the style (after many sketches), and I found a manufacturer, fabric, story, marketing—every detail. I learned the complexity of owning a business: You had to do everything. I was so excited when I got my 500 skirts and I was able to sell 100. I still have over 300 skirts in my basement.

When I moved to Louisville, Kentucky, I returned to a regular job, and guess what? I was miserable. The standards were low, and people worked in silos. I left after a year and decided to build a workspace for fashion designers. I understood my job was not to design clothing but to help designers brand themselves.

I left my fashion venture in 2020 and went full speed with my branding agency. I had already started developing tools and using archetypes to define brands, so I called the agency "bespoke branding."

The name of my fashion business was Louisville Bespoke. *Louisville* to give homage to the city that welcomed and supported me, to the incredibly diverse set of individuals that loved fashion, and to the beauty of the place where I lived. *Bespoke* for tailored experiences, tailored conversations, and tailored branding.

Making Dreams Possible

I was raised in Venezuela and moved to the U.S. at eight. After six years in the U.S., my dreams of continuing my education in California were crushed when I found out we were returning to Venezuela. Later, I received an opportunity to return to the U.S. when my father was asked to work for a university in Illinois. But after nine months in the new city of Macomb, Illinois, my dad said: "We are moving back home." *Back home?* Again, my dream of attending college in the U.S. would not unfold as I had imagined.

Yet I felt that the United States was part of my future, part of my home, so at that moment, I tapped into what was possible in my heart. I picked myself up and asked myself: *How do I do this?* I had to dig into the vision that I had for myself. Steve Jobs said: "If you are working on something you care about, you don't have to be pushed. The vision pulls you." I sat there and looked at all my opportunities, and this was when the impossible became possible.

And somehow, the right people began to show up in my life, and I could make my dream of going to college in the U.S. happen after all. And I became famous among my family as the ultimate dream executor because it seemed that anything I set my mind to could happen. That became part of my legacy.

Questions to Ponder:
- *What do you want to be remembered for?*
- *What book would you want to leave behind?*
- *What is the impact you want to leave?*
- *Where are you going?*

Chapter 4

Trust the Guide

No individual can win a game by himself.
—Plato

Mentors come in many shapes and sizes. Mentors don't even have to be alive. They can be people you admire: gods, goddesses, real living people, as well as people who have passed away. Sometimes we do not call them mentors; we call them guides, helpers, coaches, or friends. I had many mentors in my life. People who have advised me and have made me think differently and question things.

My father has been a mentor. A rebel who believes he can change thoughts with words. My father is a writer, a mathematician, and a rebel breaking all the rules. My father taught me a few things. I could be bright even if I didn't study something like mathematics. I also learned what sort of people I did not want to be around and that I needed to follow my passion.

He was the one who said no to me when I decided to go to medical school (a short-lived idea). I didn't want to attend medical school, but my aunt (his sister) suggested it. When I decided to go to design school, my father was very supportive. He loved the arts, and we went to exhibitions, ballet, and concerts and had many friends that were artists. Although mathematics came easily to him, he knew that my passion was different from his. I now understand why I wanted to follow his trajectory, not the mathematics route but the Ph.D. route. I had been looking for the perfect Ph.D. and found the ideal Ph.D. later in my life. He never forced me to study when I was young. I was a good student because I wanted to be a good student. My parents never asked for my grades or said I had to attend university. They let me be myself. I'm so grateful for that and will always be thankful for the decision they've let me make.

My mother was another mentor. Her mentorship was of a different kind. She was nurturing and let me do whatever my heart desired. She was supportive of the many endeavors I sought, and they were many.

My mother was like Mother Mary. Her entire purpose in life was to care for others; her motivation was family and the ultimate symbol of motherhood. Like Mother Mary, she was not just our mother, but a mother to many other people.

I was the oldest of four, and when I was born, my mother would say that I cried like a fountain that never stopped running. When I turned three, all I wanted was to do homework. At three, I could read, write, and do math. My mother put me in painting lessons at four, which I loved. She taught me how to read and write and supported me in anything I wanted to do.

I remember when we moved to Merida, Venezuela, when I was sixteen. We got to design our outfits and pick our fabrics, and then the seamstress made them. I was always so upset because the seamstress did not follow my sketch. My mother decided to put me in sewing lessons so I could design and sew my own clothes. She understood me and realized that a true mentor knows you, guides you, and lets you make your own decisions.

Digging for Fame

Carolina Herrera was also born in Venezuela. She began her fashion line in her later years after moving to New York and hanging out with Mick and Bianca Jagger and Andy Warhol at Studio 54. As a child, I was fascinated with painting and drawing, and I learned how to sew with a couture seamstress when I was eighteen. I designed all my clothes and loved the unexpected creative process I encountered when sketching. Although I loved the work, I never thought I could be the next Carolina Herrera. But if I couldn't be a famous fashion designer, I decided I would go for something along the same lines that you didn't have to become famous for, like graphic design.

I traveled to the U.S. and earned my undergraduate degree in industrial design. After that, I got the best job in the world, managing projects worldwide in design leadership roles across the Procter & Gamble Company, including working on brands like Olay, SK-II, DDF,

Venus, and Oral Care. Throughout my career, I have worked on total market strategy, consumer design, product innovation, and brand identity. I led over seventy design thinking and creative brainstorming sessions across multiple countries, brands, and categories. I kept leading workshops after I left P&G, and I've now conducted over one hundred design thinking sessions. This inspired me to become a professor, teaching design thinking at the MBA level because I believed so much by then in the power of creative problem-solving and how it could change lives.

My career at Procter & Gamble ended when I moved to Louisville, Kentucky, for love. I met an amazing Brit and decided to start my own business in fashion. Opening a new business in a new place and industry you have never worked in is not for the faint of heart. I got to work and built relationships with the local population. Before I knew it, I had created Louisville Bespoke, where designers, photographers, models, and anyone who loved fashion could be part of a community. We accepted everyone and anyone who just loved style.

I was surprised when three hundred people showed up at our fashion show—people from all walks of life, and the diversity was music to my eyes. Imagine dimmed lights, dance music playing, and a long runway full of photographers. I could not believe it! I had goose bumps; I was so happy. Imagine a tall woman of color in a black off-the-shoulder top with low décolletage, exposed arms, and a full-feathered skirt cut longer in the back to form a train, carrying a small purse with an @ symbol on it and a feathered headpiece that shot into the sky. Everyone in the audience was staring at her. I was like, *Wow! Mom! Dad! I've made it!* That was a moment and a feeling no one could have predicted. From then on, I was in all the local magazines; I even made it into Forbes. I had not become Carolina Herrera, but I was showcasing the Carolina Herreras of the world.

Fame is within us. We just need to dig a little.

Questions to Ponder:
- *What do you want to be known for?*
- *Who do you admire that you want to emulate?*
- *Who do you want to be connected to?*
- *If you could have a mentor, dead or alive, who would it be?*

Chapter 5

From Brand Essence to Fame Essence

Brand is just a perception, and perception
will match reality over time.
—Elon Musk

My clients are incredible individuals. Sometimes they are fearless; other times, they question everything they have done.

We are complex human beings. We want the world to know our purpose, and then we want to hide from the world. Hiding is not an option for those of us who choose the path of impact.

When you look at Coco Chanel, Carolina Herrera, or Alexander McQueen, they didn't choose to be famous; they chose to be great at fashion design. They believed in themselves and in creating clothing that spoke without words, sang without music, and talked in silence.

When I was at Procter & Gamble, I worked with top agencies and traveled the world, launching new initiatives and working on billion-dollar brands. I was extremely fortunate to work with Sabrina Jetton. Sabrina was an expert at everything and had exceptional knowledge of archetypes and strategy. I was amazed how focusing the brand on a particular archetype helped the team rally and have a single focus on how to deliver unforgettable experiences. These archetypes allowed Sabrina and me to deliver projects faster and give the team the clarity they needed to execute with excellence.

Archetypes come from Carl Jung, an influential psychologist who established the field of analytical psychology and was known for developing the first rendition of archetypes, called the Jungian archetypes. As Dr. Saul McLeod put it: "Jungian archetypes are defined as images and themes that derive from the collective unconscious, as proposed by Carl Jung. Archetypes have universal meanings across cultures and may show up in dreams, literature, art, or religion.

Jung (1947) believes symbols from different cultures are often very similar because they have emerged from archetypes shared by the whole human race, which are part of our collective unconscious."[8]

I was intrigued by how accurate and precise the archetypes were for branding. We tested them over and over with different and personal brands, revealing a pattern. It was scary how accurate the model results were. We had no hard data, but it was clear people understood the theory, and the execution modeled universal principles for design.

So, I started the agency; I chose the name Bespoke Branding. I chose the word *bespoke* because it is an old English word meaning custom-made, as in a bespoke suit or the dealing in or producing of custom-made articles by a tailor. I started using the word when no one was using it; I even read articles about not using the word because it was outdated.

Bespoke as an agency is about having a tailored brand approach to reach your "superfan" (we'll explain who this is later) by gaining a deeper understanding of yourself to empower your brand purpose and for you to rule your space. Over the years, I've noticed that psychology, in particular Jungian psychology, plays a significant role in our earthly lives. So much so that I now don't do anything without first understanding my client's archetype.

Psychology is about human beings. We live in a world made for human beings. Psychology is bringing the unconscious to the conscious. That is the complexity of our human DNA. Our brains have so much capacity, and we only use a fraction of their ability.

---

[8] Saul McLeod, "Carl Jung's Theories: Archetypes, & The Collective Unconscious," Simply Psychology, May 21, 2018, accessed January 11, 2023, https://www.simplypsychology.org/carl-jung.html.

Ilit Raz, the founder of Joonko, was quoted as saying: "We can only consciously process 40 bits. That's 99.999996% unconscious."[9]

The more conscious we become, the more authentic we can be. We can't break our capacity to be human.

I became obsessed with these Jungian archetypes and used them to start a business with the concept of "brand essence." Brand essence is the foundation of your brand personality. I have developed and designed products my entire career. The most effective concept of building products is to treat them like people because people can relate to them. If you give a product a personality, people can have a conversation with it, relate to it, and imagine it with a life of its own.

Psychologist Abraham Maslow's *hierarchy of needs* states that five categories of human needs dictate an individual's behavior. Those are physiological, safety, love, belonging, esteem, and self-actualization needs. Maslow studied how humans intrinsically behave and what motivates them and categorized these needs to describe the patterns through which human motivations generally move. The basic needs are at the bottom of the pyramid, and as you move up, it becomes more complex. When we work through the brand essence of an individual, we start at the base of the pyramid to understand their basic needs, then move up the ladder to the more complex needs of self-actualization. We use psychology to get deep into the subconscious mind and take the veil off the conscious mind.

Fame essence is like brand essence. We begin with basic needs, and then from your more complex self-actualization needs, we create what we call a "fame blueprint," which is unique to you and which you can use to make an impact, to create "fame codes" to share your gifts with the world.

---

[9] Joonko, "You Can't Prevent Unconscious Bias from Happening, so Stop Trying To," Medium, August 23, 2017, accessed January 11, 2023, https://medium.com/@JoonkoHQ/you-cant-prevent-unconscious-bias-from-happening-so-stop-trying-to-3f7a7f20590e.

Questions to Ponder:
- *What are three values you admire about yourself?*
- *How would you define those three values?*
- *Write a short story about those three values.*

Chapter 6

From Brand Character to Fame Character

If you don't give the market the story to talk about, they'll define your brand's story for you.
—David Brier

At P&G, brand character was essential to the "brand equity pyramid." The brand equity pyramid contained the brand DNA. Some people called it the "brand house." Everything in our advertising was done with brand character in mind. Brand character represented a set of human attributes and characteristics used consistently and authentically to connect to a particular audience. It had specific qualities that defined that individual product's unique personality.

Think of your favorite movie. In *Star Wars*, for example, we have the Darth Vader personality versus the Anakin Skywalker personality. Darth Vader's characteristics are stoic, heartless, and wise. On the other hand, Anakin Skywalker's are more naïve, pure, simple, and romantic.

Movie characters need to be specific and clear so the audience can connect with them. Some characters are carefree, spirited, and youthful, and some are kind, thoughtful, and oriented toward family values. Other characters are rough, outdoorsy, and athletic; still, others are competent, successful, accomplished, and influential.

Simply put, your brand character is a unique set of attributes that consistently show up so the ideal client can relate to you. How you build a long-term relationship with your customer, consumer, client, or what we call your superfan is the most crucial factor to consider.

Fame characteristics are your superpowers that attract your superfan. This relationship between you and your superfan creates tension because your superfan is your opposite.

Tension is built between opposites, and this chemistry of opposing forces between you and your superfan makes your brand irresistible and something that stands out in a saturated market.

Questions to Ponder:
- *What movie character are you playing in real life?*
- *Define your fame character.*
- *What story do you want the NY Times to write about you?*

Chapter 7

Intro to the Five Steps to Fame

The energy of the mind is the essence of life.
—Aristotle

Fame essence is the deep understanding of who you are. This inner psychological knowing and the courage to show it to the external world will allow you to impact more people.

Your fame essence is found at the tipping point where being the former, hidden you is not an option anymore. Hiding behind the curtain of your business will not take your business to the next level. Being the best-kept secret in town is no longer aligned with who you are becoming. Fame is honorable, fame is for everyone, and if you let your fame essence show, fame is inevitable.

There are **Five Steps to Fame** that we know can take people to the long-lasting fame that spells "success." These are:

1. Know Yourself
2. Know Your Superfan
3. Know Your Tension
4. Know Your Path
5. Know Your Destination

We will dive into these steps later on in the book, so you can understand your niche on the journey to fame.

Differentiation comes from within. You are unique, and no one else can be who you are. Pretending to be someone you are not is an exhausting waste of all the amazing talents you alone have to offer. The formula is simply to know who you are, know who your superfan is, and make a difference in your work with your specific brand of magic.

Once we understand what sets us apart, we can take on the world. You will always come back to who you are. When you look at the face value of a business that didn't work for you, you will quickly conclude that the reason behind it was that you were not attracting enough clients.

And if you look deeper, you'll see that the business did not attract those clients because you did not embrace your authenticity, the core of who you are. When you know who you are and freely share it, you will be unstoppable, and opportunities will come to you with little effort. No one can take away what makes you *you*.

Questions to Ponder:
- *What makes you unique?*
- *What do you do better than your competitors?*
- *Why do you do what you do?*

Chapter 8

The Fame Universe

Fame for me is not external; it's internal. So, I've been famous for a long time.
—Lady Gaga

Here's a chart with all the definitions in the fame universe.

Fame Economy	Fame economy is based on the power to communicate on a human level, the ability to authentically and transparently communicate a product's purpose, mission, and vision. The person is the driver of the sale or expansion of the company or organization.
Fame Character	Fame character represents a universal pattern of behavior. Everyone has such a psychological type, and knowing your universal type helps you find the essence of who you are.
Fame Essence	Your fame essence is the intrinsic nature of who you are, which determines your character.
Fame Leadership	Fame leadership is the expression of your brand personality, showcasing your authentic voice and offering guidance and insight to those around you.
Fameology	Fameology is the study of fame. Fame is the state of being known or recognized by many people because of your achievements, skills, and gifts.

The Levels of Fame[10]	Level 1—Fame is in our DNA because it's in our biological makeup to birth the next generation. Level 2—We tie ourselves to a cause greater than ourselves. Level 3—We create something we can attribute to our name, such as writing a book, making music, or developing a new product.
Fame Blueprint	The fame blueprint lets you see all the elements needed to define your brand before you begin. One of the most challenging parts of being an entrepreneur is feeling confident about your strategy and brand execution.
Fame Code	A fame code is a system of words, letters, figures, and symbols used to represent your fame character, especially for personal branding. The fame code delivers your unique message and the brand's meaning.
Luxury Fame	Being a celebrity in a niche market with the ability to be anonymous when you want to be.

[10] As coined by Torund Bryhn.

Fame Thinking	Fame thinking is a non-linear, iterative process for teams to understand users, challenge assumptions, reframe problems, and create innovative solutions to prototype and test. A fame-thinking approach establishes a methodology and a unifying language for how organizational disciplines interact and collaborate, applying creativity and leading to better and faster solutions.
Fame Method	The fame method is a systematic process to achieve brand excellence. The fame method includes understanding your fame essence, discovering your unique fame character, delighting your superfan, discovering your brand positioning, and executing with excellence.

Stepping into Your Purpose

After I left the big corporate world, I took some risks that some would say hadn't paid off. One of those risks was going into business for myself.

As I described earlier, I moved to Kentucky and created Louisville Bespoke, which was successful in many ways but flopped economically. What I mean is I made that business famous for creating local fashion shows that were high-end, entertaining, and diversified in every way, but it never made money. But was that really a failure? After all, I learned so much about connections, relationships, and empathy, which was worth every penny of the initial investment.

I knew I could keep going because I was doing everything myself. The truth is, I didn't know how to delegate, which meant I got sick for days after each big show, but I didn't care because it would fill my soul whenever I saw the excitement on people's faces.

In many people's eyes, I was a failure. I took a financial risk and lost it all, but everything I learned in those years was worth millions. I now see risk as a stepping stone into purpose.

I tried working at an advertising agency after corporate life and found that I wasn't cut out for that world. I had worked with many famous agencies when I was at P&G, and from that, I knew it would be challenging, but the problem was that I didn't love the work; it felt superfluous and not very creative to me, and I only lasted a year.

When I started my own business, I protected myself at first by being a consultant. Consultants come in and out and just need to give their strategies and ideas to move the business forward. The problem is that the business can decide to use your ideas or not, and you never get to see anything executed. I was determined *not* to call myself an agency because I thought I would have to be like the agencies I knew and the one I had worked at, and I could easily fail.

Eventually, I faced those fears, however, and decided to start a boutique agency, Bespoke Branding, that would focus on personal branding and creative strategies learned in part from my previous struggles. I set meaningful expectations with each of my clients, and

I also became their partner so that what I did could be seen by others, and I'd be solely responsible for it. I now love my job, and I love seeing my clients soar.

If I hadn't taken those risks earlier and learned from them, I wouldn't be here now.

Questions to Ponder:
- *What is your purpose?*
- *What is holding you back from accomplishing your purpose?*
- *What are you proud of?*

Chapter 9

Fame Is About Self-Awareness

Tenacity: The quality of being very determined; persistent forward momentum with a game plan; to never stop trying to achieve a goal, even in the face of seemingly insurmountable odds.
—Dictionary Definition

There have been many tests and trials in my life. My first test was to leave my country and my family. The second test was to leave my job at a big corporation. My third test was to let go of what I most feared (writing).
—Yamilca Rodriguez

Self-Imposed Limitations

People think that becoming famous for your actions can be done without self-awareness. It is believed that someone will see your genius, and they will take on all the work, and you can sit pretty until it's all done and ready to launch you into the world of fame. I thought this way myself. I had this genius idea, and I thought everyone would see it and I would become famous just like that.

The hard work starts with mindset and mindset alone. I have many clients who can't see their potential and constantly complain about how the process will not work.

When I started my business, I thought I would become known in months. I thought if I launched something, I would sell it right away. I learned the hard way that it wasn't as simple as "if you build it, they will come."

I noticed I had mindset issues around my worth and how I valued my work. When I saw that selling wasn't easy, I began devaluing my work and sold it for nothing. I had to work on that with a coach to help me understand I had something valuable to offer and that I had to help others through the journey of being able to see that for themselves, about their own gifts.

Once I managed to break through the barrier of self, I was able to grow my business exponentially. But it wasn't about the theory or my expertise; it was about learning the value of my work and valuing myself as an individual.

Introspection takes as long as it takes, weeks or years, depending on your level of awareness. It took me about a year, but once I understood it was all in my head, I could see a world of possibilities. But most importantly, when I saw my clients' opportunities, I could see how they could impact the world and how I could help them get out of their own way, and that was more rewarding than I could have ever imagined.

Questions to Ponder:
- *What have been three defining moments in your life?*
- *What are you not proud of?*
- *What are three possibilities you are afraid to say out loud?*

Chapter 10

Metamorphosis

Transformation literally means going beyond your form.
—Wayne Dyer

I have denied my gifts, and my clients have also denied theirs. This is the reason why I do what I do. Everyone has it in them to do something they love. But I know that you cannot do this for others, and you can only do it for yourself.

I see the transformation in my clients every day—it's incredible. I also see it in myself every time I let go of my limiting thinking. At first, it's unconscious, and it's our job to bring it to the conscious level so we can impact the world.

We don't like change, and we will push change until we have no choice but to change or be changed. If you think about *The Hero's Journey* by Joseph Campbell, there is a process. The first step is the ordinary world, where the hero regularly experiences a lack of control. (They use this journey in most movies, by the way.) The second step is the call to adventure; the ordinary world is no longer acceptable, and the hero is ripe for change. The third step is the refusal of the call, which is when the hero is uncertain, afraid, and avoids the call. These are universal, meaning we all experience them, which is why we can connect with the hero in a movie.

My clients go through the same "hero's journey." They are living their best life, and then the question comes: "Do you want to be known for what you do?" At first, they are all in, and they freak out as it gets closer to launch. They ask themselves: "What are people going to think? Can I call myself an expert? Do I want to do all the work it takes to launch my personal brand?"

These are all valid questions. Those people who can overcome this are the few who see it through. They become known in their field, and people start to notice. I have a client who started with me a year ago. Throughout the process, she needed to figure out why she was spending time and money on her personal brand. She loved it, but needed to figure out if it was working. The other day she called me all excited and said people recognized her brand. A very well-known individual had told her she loved her brand and what it stood for.

After our personal brand is executed, we must do three things: 1. Consistency: Start by defining your brand to yourself. 2. Visibility: Once you've defined your message, you must be as visible as possible. 3. Frequency: Frequency is the third aspect of creating a personal brand. Decide and stick to it!

The process of metamorphosis is simple. It brings the unconscious to the conscious so you can transform and be who you have always been meant to be.

Questions to Ponder:
- *What is your ordinary world?*
- *What is your call to adventure?*
- *What would you describe as your refusal of the call?*

Chapter 11

Hell Yes!

If it's not a 'Hell Yes!' then it's a 'Hell No!' It's that simple.
—Elizabeth Cogswell Baskin

How do you accomplish your goals? If I give 20 percent to a plan, I can complete it. Suppose the destination is a wicked plan. You may need to give it 100 percent. Suppose you give the goal 30, 40, or 80 percent. It doesn't work that way. You must be 100 percent in to achieve greatness, whatever greatness means to you.

When I worked at Procter & Gamble, I was introduced to Sabrina about two years into my career. We worked together for years, and I've learned so much from her. She is the most brilliant woman I have ever met. She taught me everything I know about archetypes and introduced me to the book *The Hero and the Outlaw*. That book was a game-changer for me. In it, authors Carol S. Pearson and Margaret Mark are quoted as saying, "A brand's meaning—how it resonates in the public heart and mind—is a company's most valuable competitive advantage. And still, few companies really know how brand meaning works, how to manage it, and how to use brand meaning strategically. This groundbreaking book provides the illusive and compelling answer. Using studies drawn from the experiences of Nike, Marlboro, Ivory, and other powerhouse brands, the authors show that the most successful brands are those that most effectively correspond to fundamental patterns in the unconscious mind known as **archetypes**."[11]

The book has changed my life, and I would not be here today without its teachings. Carol

---

[11] Margaret Mark and Carol Pearson, *The Hero and the Outlaw: Building Extraordinary Brands through the Power of Archetypes* (New York: McGraw-Hill, 2001).

Pearson spent over three decades developing systematic psychology frameworks and applying them to business and education. Similarly, Margaret Mark has worked on many household names and leverages archetypes to build successful brands.

The book states, "Understanding and leveraging archetypal meanings—that is, defining the soul of your brand and then expressing it in a way that taps into universal feelings and instincts—are the key prerequisites to effective marketing in today's intensely competitive and complex environment. When these deep psychic imprints are understood and employed, brands not only gain meaning, but companies can also gain market share and increase shareholder value."[12]

The more clients I serve, the more I use the method, and the more I can testify to its power. At the beginning of my archetype journey, I used the book daily. I was using the information in the book as my brand bible. I was using it with my brand teams. I would start every project with the team and ask them what the brand archetype was for them. The method was groundbreaking because if everyone selected the same archetype, I knew it would be easy to establish our strategy. On the other hand, if they were different, aligning the team and accomplishing the plan would take more work.

After I left P&G, I decided to use the method for personal branding. More and more people wanted to become a brand, and I had been using it for products and turning products into people with characters, but it was much easier for actual people.

I started to notice that the way Pearson had established the archetypes in the quadrants needed to shift. At the time, Sabrina needed to figure out why certain archetypes were in certain quadrants. She went back and looked at the Myers-Briggs Type Indicator and noticed that if she shifted the archetypes in the quadrants and reconfigured the model, it solved the problem. She tested it, and I tried the new model with my clients, which worked perfectly.

_____

[12] Margaret Mark and Carol Pearson, *The Hero and the Outlaw: Building Extraordinary Brands through the Power of Archetypes* (New York: McGraw-Hill, 2001).

In 2020, Sabrina and I went to Bali for a retreat I was hosting. I discovered a second aspect of the model, the opposite of what I call the superfan. As Sabrina explained the model and how the opposites worked, I had a revelation. I concluded that if the opposite of one archetype was the ideal client, then the opposite of that was the superfan. For the client that loved everything you sold, the conclusion would be to write to the opposite regarding offers and sales strategy.

This was a significant breakthrough because it has allowed me to help my clients understand their superfans and how to attract them. People think their superfan is them, but it's not. Let me tell you why. If your superfan was you, then your superfan could say, "I can do that. That's not hard." But if your superfan is your opposite, there would be no argument; you would be the answer to their problems.

My life is now completely different. I've started writing content and using it with clients, and the model works. I will always be grateful for Sabrina, who shared Pearson's book with me, and her relentless passion for solving problems.

Is your plan a HELL YES?

Questions to Ponder:
- *What is your goal today?*
- *What is your goal for the next five years?*
- *What is your goal for the next ten years?*

Chapter 12

Finding Your Fame Essence

The privilege of a lifetime is being who you are.
—Joseph Campbell

Becoming famous starts with you. How do your market yourself? The first step in your fame journey is to find the essence of what makes you tick and tell the world about it. It is about branding you, the person.

A strong indicator of how this influences current trends is that Google's search volume for "personal brand" has grown over 4X in recent years and is now seen as a critical component of consumers' purchasing decisions.[13]

The pursuit of discovering your true self is an ever-growing multi-billion industry with anticipated global growth at an average rate of 6.9% from 2022 to 2030.[14] Moreover, influencer marketing focusing on individuals fronting the product is projected to grow by 33.4% from 2022 to 2030.[15] This segment growth can be attributed to the growing emphasis among individuals on the self—to improve and understand the need to focus on themselves to grow.

Interestingly, regardless of age, gender, geographic location, job title, or income, 67% of

---

[13] "Trends in Personal Branding," Brand Builders Group, accessed December 26, 2022, accessed January 11, 2023, https://brandbuildersgroup.com/study/.

[14] "Personal Development Market Size Report, 2020-2027," Grand View Research, n.d., accessed January 11, 2023, https://www.grandviewresearch.com/industry-analysis/personal-development-market.

[15] The global influencer marketing platform market size was valued at USD 10.39 billion in 2021. It is expected to expand at a compound annual growth rate (CAGR) of 33.4% from 2022 to 2030.

ALL Americans "would be willing to spend more money on products and services from the companies of founders whose personal brand aligns with their own personal values."[16] If you are not convinced, trust is the first factor to invest in when finding your fame essence. Americans expect a person to front products or services, and 82% of Americans agree companies are more influential if their founder or executives have a personal brand they know about, trust, and follow.

So, if you are a CEO and want to grow your company, the process is to select leaders or experts from your company, invest in finding their essence, and create a plan that will help take their traits to build the company.

With the growth of the fame economy, it is natural that personal branding is key and the first step to finding your fame essence.

Why Fame Essence?
I fell in love with archetypes and saw the potential for creating a comprehensive model for people to understand their personal brand.

As I mentioned before, I became obsessed with the book *The Hero and the Outlaw* and the concept of using it for brand development. There were patterns that we began to notice and how brands could influence a company's culture.

Archetype theories and quizzes are everywhere. Personality tests are a dime a dozen. I am a personality test junkie. I studied *Enneagram*, *StrengthsFinder*, *Myers-Briggs*, and many others. Many of these personality tests did not work for branding. I had been studying and using archetypes for many years, so I decided to use them to create a simple test people could take to brand themselves clearly and consistently.

Personality tests are not new. Hippocrates used personality science for his clients.

---

[16] Richard Carufel, "Trends in Personal Branding: When Brand Aligns with Values, Most Americans Will Spend More," Agility PR Solutions, January 12, 2022, accessed January 11, 2023, https://www.agilitypr.com/pr-news/public-relations/trends-in-personal-branding-when-brand-aligns-with-values-most-americans-will-spend-more/.

Personality science has been around for decades. Archetypes are universal symbols and images derived from the collective unconscious, proposed by Carl Jung. It's the way our brain takes in information and drives human behavior.

The way the system works is simple: There are twelve archetypes. Once you find your specific archetype, that becomes the personality you use to define, inform, and deeply understand your brand strategy. Each archetype creates tension with a different archetype, which we call your superfan. Understanding your archetype and its opposite will give you the clarity to define your messaging strategy. You may feel a connection to some people more than others. You may find that your brand personality is warm, sweet, and kind, or maybe supportive, nurturing, and caring.

You can take the test to find out your archetype here: https://brandquiz. bespokebranding.io/

Questions to Ponder:
- *What is your archetype?*
- *What is the story of your archetype?*
- *How would you define your character based on your archetype?*

Chapter 13

The Twelve Dinner Guests

Guest List
Ruler and Host of Dinner Party: Jeff Bezos
Sage: Denzel Washington
Creator: Natalie Portman
Lover: Marilyn Monroe
Caregiver: Emma Thompson
Girl Next Door: Jennifer Aniston
Magician: Nelson Mandela
Performer: Lucille Ball
Outlaw: Angelina Jolie
Hero: Serena Williams
Innocent: Jennifer Garner
Explorer: Ewan McGregor

You Are Invited.
The reward for creating people's personal brands is more than I could have ever imagined.
Having an impact on people's brands is more than I could ever have asked for.
—Yamilca Rodriguez

Creating this method has been a long and challenging road for me. At the beginning of the journey, it was me not trusting myself. Now, it's been very fulfilling to see what I have been able to do, and I'm grateful for the ones I have been able to support.

Let's imagine a dinner party to which twelve guests are invited, each with a particular character. The story uses dead and alive characters to define a particular archetypical personality. This story is completely imagined, and each character is only defined by an archetypical make-up.

Marilyn Monroe (Lover) shows up at the dinner party, and she is fashionably late. She's wearing a sheer long gown hugging her body. The dress has 3,000 crystals, and underneath it is a breathless Marilyn. Everyone else watches her enter the room as she walks in, and all heads turn to look at her remarkable beauty. She says hi with a sincere smile and makes that heart-to-heart connection with everyone there. Her passion, emotional intelligence, and compassion are felt in the room.

Jeff Bezos decides to take on the mic and introduce the rest of the guests to Marilyn. Although everyone knows Marilyn Monroe, and she needs no introduction, Jeff takes control of the situation and makes his stand. He is an assertive, in-charge, and dominant man. He takes the microphone and delivers an eloquent speech.

As everyone goes back to their conversations, Ewan McGregor (Explorer) turns to Natalie Portman (Creator) and tells her all about the adventures he's had on his motorcycle. Natalie finds the talk interesting and notices Ewan is spontaneous, independent, and self-reliant. As she compares herself to him, she sees herself as more precise, rigorous, and inventive. She admires Ewan but can never see herself being so spontaneous and curious about the world.

In the other corner of the room, Jennifer Aniston (Girl Next Door) is talking to Jennifer

Garner (Innocent). Aniston tells Garner about the connections she has made in the last year. Especially her friends from *Friends* and how she still speaks to them and has nurtured these relationships. Aniston is a friendly, accepting, and inclusive woman. Garner sees how she could be more like Aniston, but she sees herself as more reserved, intentional, and romantic. Garner talks about her dream home and where she thinks of moving in the next few years. Aniston thinks Garner is a bit idealistic but enjoys the conversation and wishes to see the house once it's all built.

As everyone enters the dining room, Lucille Ball (Performer) sits next to Serena Williams (Hero). You can tell from a distance they're having an entertaining conversation. Lucille is very animated, and you can tell by her mannerisms that she is living in the moment. Lucille is playful, witty, and having fun. Serena looks beautiful and strong. You can tell she is motivated by how Lucille challenges her with her questions. Serena is self-reliant, driven, and determined to keep the conversation animated and engaging. The two women are having the time of their lives.

At the other end of the table, Emma Thompson (Caregiver) is talking to Denzel Washington (Sage). Emma is telling Denzel all about her daughter's life and achievements. She is a very supportive, nurturing, and empathetic woman. Denzel looks intent and is moved by Emma's caring heart. Denzel is methodical, wise, and knowledgeable. He is intrigued by Emma's motherly side. They know each other from the entertainment world, but they've never had a heart-to-heart conversation about life until now.

When the dinner is over, and everyone is headed to the living room for their final goodbyes, Angelina Jolie (Outlaw) and Nelson Mandela (Magician) are discussing world issues. Angelina is telling Mandela how she feels about the Ukrainian war and how this has affected everyone around her in a devastating way. She believes bold decisions need to be made about the matter. Mandela agrees and tells her about his vision for humanity at large. Angelina, a bold, spirited, risk-taking woman, is focused on breaking convention and bringing new ways of thinking to the conversation. Mandela, an insightful, dynamic, and magnetic man, knows that change is the root of the matter. He is very intrigued by Angelina's point of view and knows that she will change the world for the better.

The dinner was a complete success, and all the guests are excited to have another reunion soon.

Questions to Ponder:
- *What guest do you feel more connected to?*
- *What story would you tell about your character if you were at the dinner party?*
- *Who would you invite to your own dinner party?*

Chapter 14
The Fame Character Defined

The fame character is created based on a personality match with celebrities. These celebrities serve to simplify the concept. Human beings are not one-dimensional; we all have one primary archetype and a secondary archetype. You may find other archetypes that fit the celebrity personality, but we focus on their primary archetype to understand people's motivations.

The essence of our character is universal, and gender does not play out in the significance of the results. We tend to stereotype roles. These characters come from movies, and we use them based on their roles in other stories from the past.

Not sure how to go about defining your brand character? Here is the link to our quiz: https://brandquiz.bespokebranding.io/

If you prefer to do the quiz right here in the book, a version of it is available below.

The collective unconscious defines brands. The first thing to do is think of yourself as a brand or as the person you truly are. Please select only ONE color. You may think to yourself, *But I have all four characteristics: I'm caring, I'm independent, I'm rigorous, and I'm transformative*. Yes, you are probably right. For this exercise, please select the ONE color that truly defines you.

SELECT ONE COLOR

BELONGING–WE EXIST TO BRING PEOPLE TOGETHER!
CARING, RELATIONSHIPS, AND HUMAN CONNECTION

INDEPENDENT–WE EXIST TO CHART NEW TERRITORY AND ASK TOUGHER QUESTIONS!
SIMPLICITY, ACHIEVEMENT AND INDEPENDENCE

STABLE–WE EXIST TO BRING STABILITY AND REASSURANCE TO THE WORLD!
CONTROL, RIGOR, AND ANALYSIS

DYNAMIC–WE EXIST TO BRING REVOLUTION AND FUN TO THE WORLD!
TRANSFORMATION, CONVICTION, AND JOY

Question #1. How would you define your brand? Select one color: Green, red, blue, or yellow. (Yes, only one!)

Now, go to the color you selected and choose the quote that best describes you as a person.

SELECT ONE QUOTE FROM THE COLOR YOU SELECTED ON THE PREVIOUS PAGE

BELONGING
WE EXIST TO BRING PEOPLE TOGETHER!

1. "Beauty is whatever gives you joy"
2. "I'll be there for you"
3. "All people are created equal"

STABLE
WE EXIST TO BRING STABILITY AND REASSURANCE TO THE WORLD!

1. "Power isn't everything. It's the only thing."
2. "The best way to know the future is to create it"
3. "The truth will set you free"

INDEPENDENT
WE EXIST TO CHART NEW TERRITORY AND ASK TOUGHER QUESTIONS!

1. "Don't fence me in"
2. "Here I come to save the day"
3. "Keep it simple keep it honest"

DYNAMIC
WE EXIST TO BRING REVOLUTION AND FUN TO THE WORLD!

1. "Where there is a will. There is a way."
2. "It's my way or the highway"
3. "If I can't dance, I don't want to be part of your revolution"

Question #2. Go to the color you selected above and select one quote.

You have now identified your fame character!

Welcome to the journey of personal branding. Personal branding is not a thing. It's a feeling.

Questions to Ponder:
– *Can you describe the feeling you have about this character?*
– *Can you write a story about how this character is represented in your life?*
– *What are the five attributes you would give to this character?*

Chapter 15

The Lover Brand

LOVER

BEAUTY IS WHATEVER GIVES YOU JOY

Passionate ⓘIndulgent ⓘInstinctive ⓘEmotional ⓘCompassionate

The Lover brand's promise is about human connections, compassion, and building intimate relations. This brand wants to belong to something bigger than just a product or service. They want to see your vulnerabilities.

Sex is a part of nature. I go along with nature.
—Marilyn Monroe

Marilyn Monroe is one of the most significant sex symbols in pop culture history. She did not have to work hard at being desirable. Lovers surround themselves with people and things they love. Lovers want to give love and to be loved. Marilyn famously said in an interview in 1952 that she wore "five drops of Chanel No. 5" and nothing else in bed. "I don't want to say nude," she said, "but it's the truth." It reveals the indulgent side of Marilyn. The Lover needs to be attractive to others, and their fear is being undesirable. Marilyn wanted to be desired, and she wanted to be loved more than anything else. For the Lover, "beauty is whatever gives you joy."

The Lover Fame Five-Senses Framework:
Lover's Archetype Quote: "Beauty is whatever gives you joy."
Lover's Motivation: Beauty
Lover's Need: To be attractive
Lover's Fear: Being undesirable
Lover's Behavior: Surround themselves with people and things they love, try to become more attractive to others, try to please others.

To understand the Lover fully as a brand, let's take a look at the inspiration for their logo/icon, message, music, and movies. This will give us a 360-view of their fame character. You now have a clear path to your brand when you are ready to execute.

Logo/Icon:
  – *Rich, instinctual, attractive*

Message:
  – *Love and live.*
  – *Open up, let go of control, and feel fully alive.*
  – *Dare to sit in your darkness, to find the ever-shining jewel of being fully alive within.*
  – *Dare to dive deep into self-love.*

Music:
- *Whitney Houston*
- *Shania Twain*
- *Adele*
- *Celine Dion*

Movies:
- *Ghost*
- *Titanic*
- *Vicky Cristina Barcelona*
- *Secretary*

Scent:
- *Rose, jasmine, bergamot, and patchouli*

The Lover feels compassion and a desire for genuine closeness with others and is often praised by those around them. Their primary motivation centers on intimacy.

How Does the Lover Brand Build Tension?
The Lover delivers on passion, connection, and indulgence. As the brand grows and builds tension, it should bring adventure, authenticity, and independence (Explorer). The opposite of the Lover is the Explorer.

If you are the Lover fame character:
1. Write three Lover brand values and describe them in detail.
2. Write three Explorer customer values and describe them in detail.

Chapter 16

The Caregiver Brand

CAREGIVER

I'LL BE THERE FOR YOU

Helpful ⓘ Responsible ⓘ Empathetic ⓘ Nurturing ⓘ Supportive

The Caregiver brand's promise is about relationships, support, and caring for others. This brand brings a deep understanding of connection through empathy and nurturing. It has a sense of responsibility that people can't get anywhere else.

> *Family is the center of everything for me. But family is about connection, not necessarily about blood ties, and about extended family—and extending family.*
> —*Emma Thompson*

For Caregivers, family is everything, and this doesn't have to be their blood relatives; it can be anyone with whom they become close. *Emma Thompson*'s passion project was the Nanny McPhee films. "It goes back 15 years—I started work on Nanny McPhee long before I had Gaia, so everyone who thought I was writing a children's film because I'd had a baby was wrong," she said in an article written in The Guardian in 2010. "Even now, when things are bad, I remember the birth process. I can transport myself back to that moment when Gaia was born—it's like a well from which I draw strength."[17] Caregivers anticipate the needs of others, and Thompson said in that same article that bonds that are far from evident could enrich us if we are open to exploring them.

The Caregiver Fame Five-Senses Framework:
Caregiver's Archetype Quote: "I'll be there for you."
Caregiver's Motivation: Family
Caregiver's Need: To support others
Caregiver's Fear: Lack of understanding
Caregiver's Behavior: Cares about working closely with others, has a sincere concern about people's well-being and personal development

Logo/Icon:
– *Wholeness and comfort*

Message:
– *Be the best version of yourself.*
– *By doing what you love, you inspire and awaken the hearts of others.*
– *You are what you do, not what you say you'll do.*
– *Caring is just another word for **love**.*

---

[17] Joanna Moorhead, "Emma Thompson: 'Family Is about Connection,'" The Guardian, March 20, 2010, accessed January 11, 2023, https://www.theguardian.com/lifeandstyle/2010/mar/20/emma-thompson-nanny-mcphee-2.

Music:
- *Taylor Swift*
- *Carrie Underwood*
- *Martina McBride*

Movies:
- *The Fundamentals of Caring*
- *Sweet Inspirations*
- *Elizabeth's Gift*
- *I Am Potential*

Scent:
- *Fennel, sweet myrrh, frankincense, and thyme*

The Caregiver loves to work closely with people, allowing them to grow a bond and mutual respect. Caregivers have a sincere concern about people's well-being and personal development.

How Does the Caregiver Brand Build Tension?

The Caregiver delivers empathy, nurturing, and comfort. As the brand grows and builds tension, it should bring courage, determination, and competitiveness (Hero). The opposite of the Caregiver is the Hero.

If you are the Caregiver fame character:
1. Write three Caregiver brand values and describe them in detail.
2. Write three Hero customer values and describe them in detail.

Chapter 17

The Good Guy/Girl Next Door Brand

GIRL NEXT DOOR / GOOD GUY

ALL PEOPLE ARE CREATED EQUAL

Friendly ◦ Empathetic ◦ Realistic ◦ Inclusive ◦ Accepting

The Good Guy/Girl Next Door brand promise is about connecting to the tribe. This brand brings purpose and meaning by connecting social groups on common ground.

I was the girl next door, the damsel in distress, the one with the broken heart.
—*Jennifer Aniston*

We all know *Jennifer Aniston*'s story. Her brand lives on. The Girl Next Door is a character that is easy to connect to because she is empathetic and accepting. Rachel on *Friends* was spoiled but always sweet and tried to be a good friend. The Girl Next Door has a sincerity that only she can give. She sees the world full of people and is attracted to things that enable them to connect, interact, and belong. Traits for the Girl Next Door: Keep it natural, stay feminine, and embrace the classics. You always see Jennifer Aniston in a white T-shirt and jeans, the staple for the Girl Next Door look. When actors become "typecast," it's often because that is their true nature, and they do it so naturally.

The Good Guy/Girl Next Door Fame Five-Senses Framework:
Good Guy/Girl Next Door's Archetype Quote: "All people are created equal."
Good Guy/Girl Next Door's Motivation: Community
Good Guy/Girl Next Door's Need: To fit in
Good Guy/Girl Next Door's Fear: Being rejected
Good Guy/Girl Next Door's Behavior: Works to fit in with the crowd, makes others feel included, makes practical choices

Logo/Icon:
– *Connected and real*

Message:
– *Good people bring out the good in other people.*
– *Your vibe attracts your tribe.*
– *Appreciate good people; they are hard to come by.*
– *Kind people are my kinda people.*

Music:
– *Phil Collins*
– *Kool & The Gang*
– *Katrina and the Waves*

Movies:
- *The Good Girl*
- *The Devil Wears Prada*
- *Letters to Juliet*

Scent:
- *Vanilla, marjoram, mandarin green, and fennel*

The Good Guy/Girl Next Door invites excellent culture to the community, a culture of openness and transparency. The Good Guy/Girl Next Door wants to be part of the tribe, whether it's a social class, workplace culture, club, or union. They want to connect with others with purpose and meaning.

How Does the Good Guy/Girl Next Door Brand Build Tension?
The Good Guy/Girl Next Door delivers empathy, community, and pragmatism. As the brand grows and builds tension, it brings purity, simplicity, and honesty (Innocent). The opposite of the Good Guy/Girl Next Door is the Innocent.

If you are the Good Guy/Girl Next Door fame character:
1. Write three Good Guy/Girl Next Door brand values and describe them in detail.
2. Write three Innocent customer values and describe them in detail.

Chapter 18

The Explorer Brand

EXPLORER

DON'T FENCE ME IN

Inquisitive ▪ Self-reliant ▪ Spontaneous ▪ Adventurous ▪ Independent

The Explorer brand promise is about finding the way to the promised land. The brand likes to ask questions and sees possibilities in spontaneous ways. They share their adventures and individuality with the world.

Then, one day, when you least expect it, the great adventure finds you.
—*Ewan McGregor*

The Explorer sees an open road ahead of them and wants to feel independent and free. The movie *Motorcycle Diaries* depicts a journey of exploration. The main character, played by Ewan McGregor, travels over four months on a motorcycle from London through Europe, Kazakhstan, Russia, and Mongolia, then crosses the Bering Strait for the final leg of the trip through Alaska, Canada, and across America to their final destination: New York City. Along the way, he has enough adventures to last a lifetime. It's in *Ewan McGregor*'s veins to explore, discover, and feel independent and free.

The Explorer Fame Five-Senses Framework:
Explore's Archetype Quote: "Don't fence me in."
Explore's Motivation: Adventure
Explore's Need: To constantly seek
Explore's Fear: Being repetitive
Explore's Behavior: Seeks out new things, seeks cultural enrichment, strives for continual self-improvement

Logo/Icon:
– *Worldly, adventurous, experienced*

Message:
– *Just go.*
– *Travel is the most intense mode of learning.*
– *A job fills your pocket; adventure fills your soul.*

Music:
– *Rascal Flatts*
– *Johnny Cash*
– *Daft Punk*
– *Peter, Paul and Mary*

Movies:
  – *Life of Pi*
  – *Raiders of the Lost Ark*

Scent:
  – *Peppermint, rosemary, spearmint, and lime*

Explorers believe boundaries are self-created and can be transcended. They seek to expand beyond their industry knowledge and continually push the envelope to open all possibilities for growth and innovation.

How Does the Explorer Brand Build Tension?

The Explorer delivers adventure, authenticity, and independence. As the brand grows and builds tension, it brings passion, connection, and indulgence (Lover). The opposite of the Explorer is the Lover.

If you are the Explorer fame character:

1. Write three Explorer brand values and describe them in detail.
2. Write three Lover customer values and describe them in detail.

Chapter 19

The Innocent Brand

The Innocent brand promise is about faith in the world. The brand is positive and hopeful and has good core values. The Innocent are positive and value peace, ease, and simplicity.

I'm a peacemaker. I can fit into a lot of situations. I'm pretty easygoing. I have a lot of patience.
—Jennifer Garner

Jennifer Garner's brand narrative is about goodness, innocence, and, by extension, trustworthiness, making her the perfect ambassador for skincare products and credit card companies. The Innocent sees the good and right in the world and is attracted to simple, straightforward solutions. Justice and honesty are sacred to Jennifer Garner, making her reliable and romantic. Jennifer Garner is willing to work for a better world.

The Innocent Fame Five-Senses Framework:

Innocent's Archetype Quote: "Keep it simple and honest."

Innocent's Motivation: Purity

Innocent's Need: To do what's right

Innocent's Fear: Doing things wrong

Innocent's Behavior: Reads instructions, follows the rules, identifies simple, easy solutions

Logo/Icon:
- *Simple and pure*

Message:
- *Every day is a fresh start.*
- *What's meant to be will always find a way.*
- *Keep life simple.*
- *It's a good day to be happy.*

Music:
- *Puremusic*
- *Kinsey*
- *Florida Georgia Line*

Movies:
- *The Breakfast Club*
- *Before Sunrise*
- *Chocolat*
- *Almost any Hallmark movie*

Scent:

- *Fennel, thyme, vanilla, and sweet myrrh*

The Innocent has personal values and morality and is intrinsically good-natured. The desire to make everything "great" can blind them to the reality surrounding their work. Rose-colored glasses seem to be their go-to design.

How Does the Innocent Brand Build Tension?

The Innocent delivers purity, simplicity, and honesty. As the brand grows and builds tension, it brings empathy, community, and acceptance (Good Guy/Girl Next Door). The opposite of the Innocent is the Good Guy/Girl Next Door.

If you are the Innocent fame character:

1. Write three Innocent brand values and describe them in detail.
2. Write three Good Guy/Girl Next Door customer values and describe them in detail.

Chapter 20

The Hero Brand

The Hero brand promise is about determination and discipline. The brand goes beyond expectations and shares the drive to accomplish things and the courage to take risks.

Make sure you're very courageous: Be strong, be extremely kind, and above all, be humble.
—Serena Williams

Serena Williams is competitive, humble, and calm. Heroes are attracted to challenges that offer excellent opportunities to conquer, protect, and uphold. Serena Williams and her sister, Venus, have created a legacy by inspiring more African American children to play tennis, especially those from low-income areas. The sisters are dedicated to giving their time and money to the development of these children. Heroes are motivated by being able to use their talents to help others achieve their dreams.

The Hero Fame Five-Senses Framework:
Hero's Archetype Quote: "Here I come to save the day."
Hero's Motivation: Competition
Hero's Need: To receive a challenge
Hero's Fear: Being defeated
Hero's Behavior: Saves the day, works to be strong and competent, motivates others to achieve

Logo/Icon:
   – *A symbol, letter, or seal of strength*

Message:
   – *It is not who I am underneath but what I do that defines me.*
   – *Courage is resistance to fear, mastery of fear, not absence of fear.*
   – *With great power comes great responsibility.*

Music:
   – *Mariah Carey*
   – *Foo Fighters*
   – *College*
   – *"Zero to Hero," from the movie* **Hercules**

Movies:
- *Wonder Woman*
- *Hercules*
- *Star Wars*
- *The Incredibles*

Scent Inspiration:
- *Bitter orange, ginger, lemon, and black pepper*

Despite potential risks, the Hero will give their all to "make things right." They're not afraid of being the first to define the path, even if it means defeat. Heroes, of course, find favor easily with friends, keeping their cool even in difficult situations.

How Does the Hero Brand Build Tension?

The Hero delivers courage, determination, and competitiveness. As the brand grows and builds tension, it should bring empathy, nurturing, and comfort (Caregiver). The opposite of the Hero is the Caregiver.

If you are the Hero fame character:

1. Write three Hero brand values and describe them in detail.
2. Write three Caregiver customer values and describe them in detail.

RULER

POWER ISN'T EVERYTHING. IT'S THE ONLY THING.

Powerful ▫ Unflappable ▫ In-charge ▫ Demanding ▫ Dominant

The Ruler brand promise is about dominance and power and keeping things under control. They share their strength to help people with stability and growth. The Ruler brand can help others learn how to be in charge and the strategies for brand domination.

Power is not given to you. You have to take it.
—Beyoncé

Beyoncé is one of the most powerful performers in the entertainment industry. She is ambitious, driven, and in charge, and she loves to set and accomplish goals. Rulers see the best in the world and have very high expectations of themselves and others. Beyoncé has played every card right to become the most powerful woman in music. The Ruler controls the situation, seeks success, and creates predictable and stable experiences to win.

The Ruler Fame Five-Senses Framework:
Ruler's Archetype Quote: "Power isn't everything. It's the only thing."
Ruler's Motivation: Power
Ruler's Need: To be in control
Ruler's Fear: Losing control
Ruler's Behavior: Takes control of the situation, creates predictable and stable experiences, seeks success and prosperity

Logo/Icon:
- *Upscale monogram, seal of authority*

Message:
- *Make it happen.*
- *There is no force more powerful than a woman determined to rise.*
- *Success is no accident.*

Music:
- *Henry Purcell*
- *William Walton*
- *Gordon Jacob*
- *John Ireland*

Movies:
- *The Windsors*
- *The Tudors*
- *The Crown*

Scent:
- *Sandalwood, musk, damask rose, geranium, neroli, and cedar*

The Ruler is all about control, control, and more control. Rulers create order, systems, and environments that they believe are needed to stay winning! Rulers come in all shapes and sizes, and though they all tend to be similarly autocratic, the outcome of their brand will vary from person to person and place to place.

How Does the Ruler Brand Build Tension?
The Ruler is powerful, stable, and predictable. As the brand grows and builds tension, it should deliver insight, adoption, and transformation (Magician). The opposite of the Ruler is the Magician.

If you are the Ruler fame character:
1. Write three Ruler brand values and describe them in detail.
2. Write three Magician customer values and describe them in detail.

SAGE

THE TRUTH WILL SET YOU FREE

Analytical ● Knowledgeable ● Intelligent ● Wise ● Methodical

The Sage brand promises knowledge. The brand is about sharing information gained over time. People go to the Sage because they are a source of knowledge and can do it better than anyone else.

Luck is where opportunity meets preparation.
—Denzel Washington

Denzel Washington is knowledgeable, critical, and pragmatic, verbalizing clear expectations and feedback. He is wise, organized, and methodical and enjoys engaging in debates and making tough decisions. Denzel Washington has a BA in drama and journalism, which means he rigorously studies every role he plays and reflects on each scene. The Sage sees the world as information and loves to learn and gain wisdom. The Sage wants the truth. We live in an era of "too much information," Washington said, adding that one consequence is that the pressure on the media to be the first to report something is greater than the need for it to be true. "So what a responsibility you all have—to tell the truth," he added, speaking to a group of reporters on the red carpet. The Sage studies information to gain an understanding of the world.

The Sage brand promise is about building knowledge over time and sharing it.

The Sage Fame Five-Senses Framework:
Sage's Archetype Quote: "The truth will set you free."
Sage's Motivation: Wisdom
Sage's Need: To analyze
Sage's Fear: Not knowing
Sage's Behavior: Studies information to gain knowledge, uses intelligence and analysis to understand the world, can study issues forever

Logo/Icon:
  – *Analytical, innovative, smart*

Message:
  – *Intelligence will never stop being beautiful.*
  – *Thinking is difficult; that's why most people judge.*
  – *The eyes are useless when the mind is blind.*
  – *No man is free who is not master of himself.*

Music:
  – *Tech house music*
  – *Hi-tech trance, Transience Mix*
  – *Underground house music*

Movies:
- *Inception*
- *The Matrix*
- *Tron*
- *Ex Machina*

Scent:
- *Clary sage, bergamot, eucalyptus, holy basil, and cardamom*

The Sage has the desire to discover the truths of the world. Their primary goal is to expand their knowledge and create things that move society forward. They have a general knack for learning about their environment and who they are.

How Does the Sage Brand Build Tension?
The Sage is analytical, knowledgeable, and methodical. As the brand grows and builds tension, it brings playfulness, joy, and wit (Performer). The opposite of the Sage is the Performer.

If you are the Sage fame character:
1. Write three Sage brand values and describe them in detail.
2. Write three Performer customer values and describe them in detail.

The Creator Brand

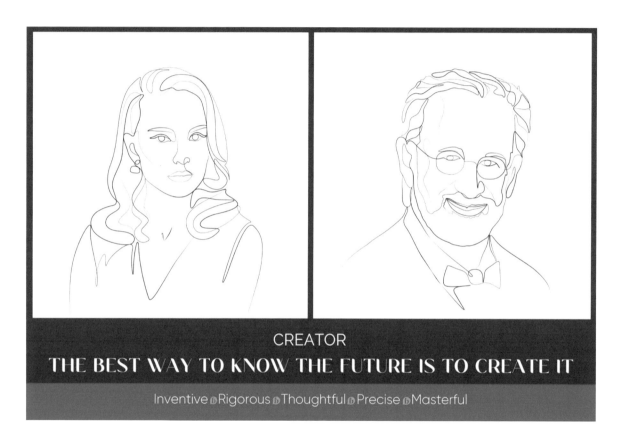

CREATOR

THE BEST WAY TO KNOW THE FUTURE IS TO CREATE IT

Inventive ⓘⓝ Rigorous ⓘⓝ Thoughtful ⓘⓝ Precise ⓘⓝ Masterful

The Creator brand promise is about precision and craftsmanship.

I don't dream at night, I dream at day, I dream all day. I am dreaming for living.
—Steven Spielberg

Steven Spielberg's key characteristics are rigor and focus. He is very inventive and masterful at his art. The Creator is attracted to things that enable them to build, prototype, and refine. Spielberg works hard and is persistent, and he can sometimes be a bit of a perfectionist. Learning to be assertive has served him well throughout his life. The Creator needs to create enduring value. They are focused on honing their skill at creating beautiful things.

The Creator Fame Five-Senses Framework:

Creator's Archetype Quote: "The best way to know the future is to create it."

Creator's Motivation: Perfection

Creator's Need: To create enduring value

Creator's Fear: Never achieving greatness

Creator's Behavior: Develops skills, invents new ways to do things, creates beautiful things

Logo/Icon:

- *Architectural, innovative, artistic*

Message:

- *Imagination rules the world.*
- *I was created to create.*

Music:

- *Classical music*
- *String quartet*
- *David Garrett*
- *Coldplay*

Movies:

- *The Pianist*
- *Chocolat*
- *A Craftsman*

Scent:
- *Bergamot, lemon, and frankincense*

The Creator is an artist at heart and disciplined in their craft. Looking to both inspire and be inspired, their imaginative nature can lead them in many directions, with self-expression and creativity at the foundation of their endeavors.

How Does the Creator Brand Build Tension?
The Creator is rigorous, precise, and structured. As the brand grows and builds tension, it brings disruption, boldness, and spirit (Outlaw). The opposite of the Creator is the Outlaw.

If you are the Creator fame character:
1. Write three Creator brand values and describe them in detail.
2. Write three Outlaw customer values and describe them in detail.

Chapter 24

The Magician Brand

MAGICIAN

WHERE THERE IS A WILL. THERE IS A WAY.

Adaptive • Insightful • Persuasive • Dynamic • Magnetic

The Magician brand promise is about transformation, adaptation, and change. The Magician brand brings a sense of transformation to everything it touches. The brand brings something new and innovative to the world. It's never static; it's always moving and dancing with systems and patterns.

Education is the most powerful weapon which you can use to change the world.
—Nelson Mandela

Magicians want to change the world for the better. That certainly applies to the work of leader *Nelson Mandela* in South Africa. He was a visionary like no other, and he made magic literally and figuratively. They called it the "Mandela Magic." Mandela personified how the human spirit could triumph over hate and evil in the face of seemingly insurmountable odds. He was about change and transformation, and he also understood the world's systems and could combine them to achieve unbelievable feats.

The Magician Fame Five-Senses Framework:
Magician's Archetype Quote: "Where there is a will, there is a way."
Magician's Motivation: Change
Magician's Need: To transform
Magician's Fear: Being undervalued
Magician's Behavior: Inquires about the world around them, sees the world as a system, achieves unbelievable feats

Logo/Icon:
- *Dynamic, flowing, adaptive*

Message:
- *If you can dream it, you can do it.*
- *Vision is the art of seeing what is invisible to others.*
- *We cannot become what we want by remaining what we are.*

Music:
- *Enya*
- *Harp songs*
- *Jennifer Haines*
- *Blue Midnight*

Movies:
- *Harry Potter*
- *The Lord of the Rings*
- *Avatar*

Scent:
- *Ylang-ylang, frankincense, and sweet orange*

Magicians are visionaries at their core. They are the movers and shakers who work hard once they set their minds on a goal. They are always looking at the newest, most significant happenings and don't mind taking a calculated risk if it means transforming an industry or eliminating an outdated practice.

How Does the Magician Brand Build Tension?

The Magician delivers insight, adoption, and transformation. As the brand grows and builds tension, it should bring power, stability, and predictability (Ruler). The opposite of the Magician is the Ruler.

If you are the Magician fame character:

1. Write three Magician brand values and describe them in detail.
2. Write three Ruler customer values and describe them in detail.

Chapter 25

The Outlaw Brand

OUTLAW

IT'S MY WAY OR THE HIGHWAY

Disruptive ① Bold ① Spirited ① Risk-taking ① Rebellious

The Outlaw brand promise is about breaking convention. The Outlaw brand revolutionizes platforms and introduces new ways to think about old systems. They share their beliefs and break all the rules!

I think we all have light and dark inside us.
—Sean Penn

Outlaws have a light and dark side. The Outlaw can be the villain in some circumstances. *Sean Penn*'s essential nature is being an Outlaw. The Outlaw tends to do humanitarian work and loves getting involved with politics. A week after the devastating 2010 earthquake in Haiti, Penn moved there. Living in a tiny tent, a Glock gun at his side for security, he dispensed medicine, carried heavy bags of rice, and swept floors. Outlaws display a mix of bravado, altruism, and daredevil recklessness. They are controversial darlings of the anti-establishment movement.

The Outlaw Fame Five-Senses Framework:
Outlaw's Archetype Quote: "It's my way or the highway."
Outlaw's Motivation: Uniqueness
Outlaw's Need: To disrupt
Outlaw's Fear: Being inconsequential
Outlaw's Behavior: Disrupts the status quo, pioneers revolutionary ideas, identifies problems, finds faults

Logo/Icon:
– *Bold, disruptive, unique*

Message:
– *Intense ideas drive performance.*
– *Feel, act, and feast.*
– *Unleash the rebel.*
– *Dare to live boldly and with full intensity.*

Music:
– *Bob Marley*
– *Prince*
– *Lady Gaga*
– *Etta James*

Movies:
- *Natural Born Killers*
- *Pulp Fiction*
- *A Clockwork Orange*

Scent:
- *Woody, spicy, and bold*

The Outlaw takes risks and does not shun what may seem like radical ideas or decisions. They inherently scoff at the notion of tradition and deeply believe in the freedom to challenge anything that doesn't align with their moral compass or beliefs of limitation.

How Does the Outlaw Brand Build Tension?
The Outlaw is disruptive, bold, and spirited. As the brand grows and builds tension, it brings rigor, precision, and structure (Creator). The opposite of the Outlaw is the Creator.

If you are the Outlaw fame character:
1. Write three Outlaw brand values and describe them in detail.
2. Write three Creator customer values and describe them in detail.

Chapter 26

The Performer Brand

PERFORMER
IF I CAN'T DANCE, I DON'T WANT TO BE PART OF YOUR REVOLUTION.
Fun-loving • Playful • Joyous • Light-hearted • Witty

The Performer brand promise is about delivering experiences. The Performer brand is fun, and the experiences it creates are ones that people can enjoy. The brand makes everything dynamic and glorious. Play, play, play! Work is play.

I don't know how to tell a joke. I never tell jokes. I can tell stories that happened to me… anecdotes. But never a joke.
—Lucille Ball

Lucille Ball was one of the greatest entertainers of all time, and she believed the secret to comedy was what she called an "enchanted sense of play."[18] The Performer sees the world as a stage and loves to experience life fully and enjoy the moment. Lucille Ball's on-screen persona was madcap and hilarious. Off-screen, she pioneered the comedy and entertainment industry, performing expertly as a businesswoman and breaking barriers for women in the industry.

The Performer always has a great time, lights up the world, and enjoys life.
The Performer Fame Five-Senses Framework:
Performer's Archetype Quote: "If I can't dance, I don't want to be part of your revolution."
Performer's Motivation: Happiness
Performer's Need: To live in the moment
Performer's Fear: Being bored
Performer's Behavior: Helps others have a great time, lights up the world, enjoys life

Logo/Icon:
– *Witty, playful, and joyous*

Message:
– *Life is a party!*
– *I just want to spend my life laughing.*
– *Admit it… Life would be boring without me.*
– *Be a Fruit Loop in a world of Cheerios.*

Music:
– *Pharrell Williams*
– *Daft Punk*
– *Janelle Monáe*
– *Taylor Swift*

---

[18] Lou Haviland, "Lucille Ball and Vivian Vance's Friendship Was Tested during This Worst Moment on 'I Love Lucy,'" Showbiz Cheat Sheet, September 22, 2020, accessed January 11, 2023, https://www.cheatsheet.com/entertainment/lucille-ball-and-vivian-vances-friendship-was-tested-during-this-worst-moment-on-i-love-lucy.html/.

Movies:
  – *The Secret Life of Walter Mitty*
  – *Dark Shadows*
  – *Alice in Wonderland*
  – *The Birdcage*

Scent:
  – *Fennel, mandarin green, marjoram, and spearmint*

Performers are always racing against time. They believe that the world is their playground. Their goal is to experience everything they can and achieve their numerous endeavors amid a fast-paced lifestyle.

How Does the Performer Brand Build Tension?

The Performer is playful, joyous, and witty. As the brand grows and builds tension, it brings analysis, knowledge, and meaning (Sage). The opposite of the Performer is the Sage.

If you are the Performer fame character:

1. Write three Performer brand values and describe them in detail.
2. Write three Sage customer values and describe them in detail.

Chapter 27

You Are Not One-Dimensional

Always remember that you are absolutely unique. Just like everyone else.
—Margaret Mead

The fame character is more accessible when looked at from a one-dimensional perspective. As human beings, we are much more complex. As we get more involved in the work, we must look at a secondary fame character. It is sometimes difficult to pinpoint a fame character because the two may be intertwined, which is normal. That is why we often can't guess our own or someone else's fame character.

Adding more flavor to our primary fame character will give us a unique and fully developed character. The magic lies in integrating both characters into our personality. In the beginning, it is simpler to take on one character. As we understand better, sprinkling in the secondary character gets easy.

Once we have our primary and secondary fame characters, we have a brand positioning. Brand positioning is critical to set yourself apart from your competition. The only way to set yourself apart from competitors is to go entirely into character and use positioning to differentiate your brand.

Imagine how many stories you can tell, how much content you can write, and how many ideas and offers you can develop by knowing your brand positioning. Brand positioning can genuinely set and resonate deeply with your superfan.

My primary fame character is the Lover, and my secondary one is the Magician. I use both characters entirely in my brand and in every way possible. The Lover in me is passionate, indulgent, and super emotional, and the Magician is magnetic, insightful, and adaptive. I'm not one or the other. They are both parts of my brand (and me), and I bring them in as needed. I can make magic literally and figuratively, and I can also surround myself with people and things I love and indulge in self-care.

Knowing Your Fame Character

Why is it so hard for us to acknowledge love for what we have created, love for who we are, including our mishaps? Once you find your true essence, your job is to exploit it. This means exploring it consistently and executing it every day. Embrace yourself, the bad and the good. Talk about the things you wouldn't ordinarily acknowledge. Love yourself and let go of the old. Old habits lead to old thinking; new habits lead to possibilities. Love and welcome your uniqueness because that is what will bring you success.

My Lover Story

I didn't want to embrace the Lover in me for the longest time; I only wanted to embrace the visionary theorist. What I had to do was embrace both fully. My fashionista was the Lover, and the strategist part of me was the Magician. The two together made me a unique individual, but I had to acknowledge and embrace both to move my unique brand into the limelight.

As a young girl, I was obsessed with dresses, shoes, and makeup. I was a girly girl. I only wanted to be a princess on Halloween, and I saw it as an opportunity to put on a fancy dress, high heels, and makeup. My mother was not one to wear makeup, so I had to be super-creative. Later, in my teenage years, I fell in love with fashion. I watched fashion shows and dreamed of being a designer. I wanted to be Carolina Herrera.

I was born in Caracas, Venezuela. I had so much fun traveling to Brazil, Argentina, and Peru when I was seven, and then my entire family moved to San Diego, California, when I turned eight. In San Diego, I had to quickly learn the language and adapt to meet new friends, which was easy for me. I surrounded myself with people and things I loved.

My family and I returned to Venezuela in my mid-teens. By then, I couldn't see myself as a fashion designer. I wanted to be Carolina Herrera, but I thought you needed to be rich to study abroad in the fashion mecca, and for me, that was Italy. I investigated the possibility, but it seemed unreachable at the time. I went on to what seemed feasible— graphic design—and from there, I found my way to industrial design. I was a creative, passionate designer. I loved creating beautiful things. I could draw, paint, and build, inventing possibilities.

I did everything and anything to make my dream of studying abroad come true. I was the oldest of four. I left home and ventured to a place where I knew no one. I was determined to succeed, and I landed in Cincinnati. I stayed with friends of my family for a week, found a job, and got myself into the top industrial design school in the country. Although I missed my family, it was easy for me to make friends and allies, and in a short amount of time, I managed to build strong relationships that helped me along the way. I knew what I wanted and always found a way to get it. I graduated magna cum laude from the University of Cincinnati. I knew I had to work three times harder than anyone else to achieve anything I put my mind to because I was a woman and Hispanic. I now see that I was also challenged because I didn't yet value my superpowers.

Once I graduated, I was hired to work at the best branding company in the world. I worked for Procter & Gamble for fifteen years, traveling the world, and I became an eternal student of human behavior. I loved speaking to thousands of people worldwide about the products I designed. I worked on billion-dollar global brands and had the resources to learn from industry experts. I completed my MBA while working.

I resisted the Lover for so long because I felt I couldn't be the intellectual person I thought I wanted to be. I felt the Lover only cared about beauty and was too emotional for this world. Embracing my true self made my unique magic shine through, and I felt empowered.

Questions to Ponder:
- *How are you unique in what you do?*
- *What is the story that differentiates you from everybody else?*
- *If you could describe what you do as a metaphor, what would it be?*

Chapter 28

Case Study: Chanel, The Power Of The Creator

In order to be irreplaceable, one must always be different.
—Coco Chanel

As a lover of fashion, I have always admired Coco Chanel.

Gabrielle Chanel was ambitious, strong, entrepreneurial, and thirsted for freedom to be herself no matter what. She challenged society and its norms. She was incredibly innovative in creating her own identity. Her fashion sense revolutionized the industry.

So, where did her desire for fame come from? Coco Chanel kept her origins a mystery. She had this uncontrollable, impulsive, rugged, and determined energy. This thirst for work and design to accomplish unbelievable feats.

Gabrielle Chanel was highly superstitious and obsessed with numbers and numerology. She had her favorite numbers and knew precisely how to use them for her brand. The most important, of course, was the number five.

Coco Chanel lived an extraordinary life. She was extremely confident and ambitious. She believed she had invented the idea of elegance. Her taste for eternity made her style a classic that would leave a legacy through her creations. She wanted to create a legend and was quoted as saying, "May my legend prosper and thrive. I wish it a long and happy life."

She was always looking for perfection. That tells me right there that her fame character can only be the CREATOR. The Creator is an artist, a writer, an innovator, and an entrepreneur. The Creator brand is not about fitting in; it's about self-expression. The Creator wants to create something that has never been there before, to create a work of art so special that it endures and goes on to achieve some sort of immortality.

Women in the 20th century were comfortable with their professional independence. Coco Chanel earned enough money, met Baron Étienne Balsan, and broke all the rules. Her superfan archetype is the Outlaw, wanting to be reached in non-traditional ways. They want things that are shocking, surprising, or just outright disturbing. The Outlaw superfan likes edgy products that allow people to kick back and feel free.

In a society dominated by men, it was logical that women would rely on those with money and influence. They used men in a way that they were not too dependent on them. Women's refusal to get married might have had to do with their ambition and desire to accomplish something.

Coco Chanel was willing to terminate her brand if it couldn't stay true to who she was. I love that about Coco—no compromise on quality. She was a true renaissance woman, authentic and fearless, so she became an icon.

How Do People Become Icons?

Quite easily. To become an icon, you must believe in something and then keep doing it repeatedly. Forming your beliefs is where the rubber hits the road. It's not like you develop new ideas. You uncover your thoughts and start reflecting on them. Coco Chanel did everything her way. She stood up for her craft and art—very different from how her predecessors did fashion, but in her unique and undeniable way. Coco Chanel's brilliance was simplicity. She understood that simplicity equaled elegance. She took a simple suit and wore it repeatedly, pointing out that all you'd ever need is an elegant suit, some pearls, and the unforgettable No. 5.

Chanel was an artist who believed in herself and never wanted to discuss the reality of her past. She dug deep, and her superpowers were to stand firm in her convictions and deliver a legacy that none could break. She knew her strengths and exploited them. Do you know yours? Are you willing to use them to become famous?

Coco Chanel did not focus on what others thought of her. Life was real. She defined luxury as freedom. Think about that for a moment. Luxury was the freedom for women to set their own beliefs and was the suit of liberty.

Chanel No. 5 is the world's most famous perfume. They say that, somewhere in the world, a bottle of Chanel No. 5 sells every fifty-five seconds.

A woman who never wears perfume has no future.

—Coco Chanel

When I think about Chanel No. 5, it gives me wings, but Chanel No. 5 is undeniably futuristic. Coco Chanel wanted women to know that they were free to be themselves. To believe they were assertive and that the scent could drive them to fame if they believed it.

The future is yours. Leave your mark and make your unforgettable scent known.

Questions to Ponder:
- *What is your power?*
- *How do you use your power?*
- *What is the feeling you get when you are in your power?*

Chapter 29

The Five Steps to Fame

The five steps to fame were developed on my journey of self-discovery. The more client assessments we did, the more we learned—and the more I learned about myself. Concepts are developed as we open up to new possibilities. This book was a possibility that I perceived as unattainable because I didn't think I had it in me to write a book.

Let's explore these steps together, starting from the very beginning.

Step 1: Know Yourself

> *Life is not a problem to be solved, but a mystery to be lived.*
> *—Joseph Campbell*

The first step in knowing yourself is to know your fame character. If you have not yet taken the survey, please stop what you are doing and take it: https://brandquiz. bespokebranding.io/

My Story
Knowing yourself is the first step to self-discovery. Talking about knowing myself makes me sound like I must have read many self-help books to discover who I was. I joke about this, but I did read many self-help books in my thirties and forties. The more I knew, the more I wanted to know. I was seeking transformation at every turn. I guess you could call me a transformation junkie. This is what got me into who I am today. I love psychology because it has changed my life, and I know it can help others.

The more you know yourself, the more you can trust your instincts. Today, I need to investigate if I don't feel good about something. Every time I ignore my instincts, I get myself into trouble. I have clients who have difficulty integrating their true nature because they are fighting their instincts and believe they must be somebody else.

You attract the right people, clients, and work. You draw your superfan. You can only attract your superfan if you live your true purpose. Once you know who you are, you are ready to attract your superfan and integrate fame into your life. There is no fear in pursuing your true purpose when you know yourself well. At this turning point, you attract what has always been yours.

A true storyteller was Joseph Campbell, a believer in archetypes and the importance of characters. We are all characters in our own stories. Joseph Campbell showed how these stories reflect the human psychological experience. He theorized, "We are all heroes struggling to accomplish our adventure. As human beings, we engage in a series of struggles to develop as individuals and to find our place in society."[19]

Procter & Gamble was a fertile ground for product development. We worked on thousands of products globally each year. Just imagine sixty-five individual brands organized into ten product categories that produce infinite ideas and concepts. I worked on many categories and brands and learned that you could not stand out if you didn't define your brand with a specific character type. Differentiation is most important when the market is saturated with products.

I was responsible for the rebranding of Scope mouthwash. Scope was originally a fresh and flirty brand focusing on good breath without the medicine taste. It was an experiential brand, but Scope had never left the 1970s. Scope was my first project when I started with Oral Care. It was given to me because they wanted to know what I could do with a brand losing market share year after year. In my years before joining Oral Care, I was in the beauty category, primarily working on innovation and future trend projects. By contrast, there was very

[19] Elizabeth Van Sickel, "The Power of Story: How Understanding Our Narrative Transforms Our Perspective," Restored Hope Counseling Blog, December 14, 2017, accessed January 11, 2023, https://www.restoredhopecounselingservices.com/blog/2017/12/14/the-power-of-story-how-understanding-our-narrative-transforms-our-perspective.

little to do with a brand like Scope that had only the short-term goal of survival, but I loved a challenge.

The challenge was that Scope loyalists were dropping like flies and new consumers found no relevance in the brand. We decided to win over consumers by carving out a place of flexibility in the category and giving Scope the brand character of an irreverent fun-starter. Our simple idea that red lipstick was a badge of courage led to the big picture that would redefine Scope and set it miles apart from its competition. This idea was fun, lighthearted, and flexible enough to make our brand iconic.

Unfortunately, the brand wasn't given the time or investment needed to become an icon. When you stop spending advertising dollars on a brand, it dies slowly. But I learned from this experience that a brand's character is one of its essential attributes. A new brand character can change everything, and the one we gave Scope was the Performer, the individual attracted to experiences that helped them live in the moment and enjoy life.

You want the world to see your brand's unique combination of skills, experience, and personality. It tells the product and service story, reflecting that unique mix of behavior, spoken and unspoken words, and attitudes. The brand's character needs to be defined in a particular way so that you or the product can bring out its unique tone of voice every time you interact with an audience. The fame character of your brand can help you define the tone of voice of your product in a super-simple and consistent manner.

Let's look at what happens when known brands use a fame character.

Corporate Fame Character Analysis
Apple behaves in the world as an Outlaw and continues to disrupt and revolutionize every industry it touches. The iPhone, Apple TV+, and MacBook Air broke convention and brought the world what it didn't know it was longing for. The company's tagline is "THINK DIFFERENT," which says it all.

Starbucks behaves in the world as an Explorer. It continues to navigate uncharted territories, new communities, and new partnerships with growers and fresh food/snack partners to entice you every day.

Tesla behaves in the world as a Creator, crafting beautiful objects of desire with the rigor and intensity that only a Creator can bring. They have brought us battery, transportation, and energy innovations, creating a truly remarkable and legendary brand.

Coca-Cola behaves in the world as an Innocent, promising paradise with a simple sip. Even if the world crumbles, everything will be okay if we can still enjoy a bottle of Coke. They have crafted a storyline that symbolizes the innocence and naivete of youth in a single trademark.

Airbnb behaves as a Good Guy/Girl Next Door, making anyone feel at home, comfortable, and fit into the place they travel. The company supports an entire network of super hosts who want to make people feel welcomed and like they belong—changing the world of hospitality from a humanitarian point of view.

Questions to Ponder:
- *What is your fame character?*
- *Describe your fame essence in detail.*
- *What movie would your fame character play? Imagine you are a screenwriter and develop a story about yourself as the lead character in a movie.*

Step 2: Know Your Superfan

The greater the tension, the greater the potential.
—Carl Jung

Your job is to know your superfan inside and out. You need to write love letters to your superfan that reflect your purpose. To attract your superfan, you need to learn their language. It is not necessarily the language of love, but a new language that you will need to integrate into your message.

Your Superfan Is Your Opposite

Carl Jung wasn't the only person discussing polarity and its power. Sir Isaac Newton stated in the Third Law of Motion, "For every action, there is an equal and opposite reaction."[20] This is all to say that the most critical element for your business is attracting and serving your superfan. We think our superfan will be someone like us; I tell you, they're not.

Your superfan is the opposite of you. Why? Because they can't do what you can. They don't know how to do what you do and need all the help they can get from you because your superfan knows they can't do what you do. They will not try to negotiate with you because they will pay whatever they have to acquire your skill.

Please stop trying to attract individuals like you and start attracting your opposite because they need you!

Look at the graph below to find your superfan. Find your fame character, and the archetype across from it is your superfan (your opposite). For example, if your fame character is the Magician, your opposite is the Ruler. Go back to the profile of the Ruler and see what language you need to use and how to serve them.

---

[20] Nancy Hall, "Newton's Laws of Motion," Glenn Research Center (NASA, October 27, 2022), accessed January 11, 2023, https://www1.grc.nasa.gov/beginners-guide-to-aeronautics/newtons-laws-of-motion/.

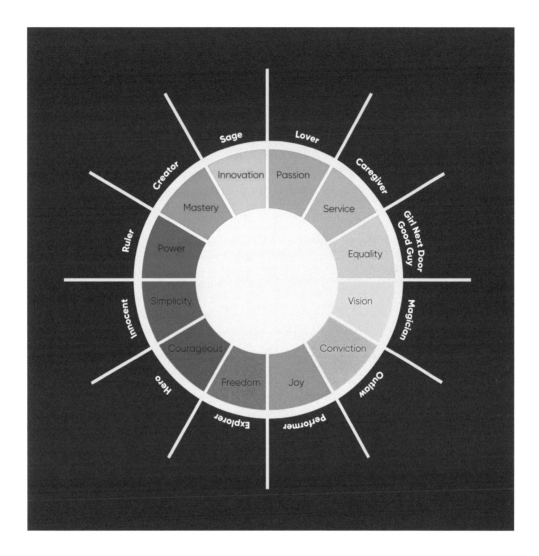

The Experience Framework Model by Sabrina Jetton. This graph lists the twelve archetypes and a one-word description for each. Directly across from each archetype is its opposite.

Questions to Ponder:
  – *Who is your superfan?*
  – *Describe your superfan.*
  – *How will you delight your superfan?*

Step 3: Know Tension

It takes confidence and guts to intentionally create tension.
—Seth Godin

The Science of Tension

I have studied the science of tension for the last fifteen years. It was introduced to me by my dear friend Sabrina Jetton, one of the most intelligent women I know. While working at P&G, I hired Sabrina to help me with a project. We created many new concepts, and six months later, we created a language of our own. We would talk about ideas that no one understood.

Over the years, I have taken those ideas and developed an entire methodology. Years after working with Sabrina, I met Torund, and we transformed that methodology into what we now call the fame method.

The fame method starts with understanding your fame character, the science of understanding yourself. Once you can internalize your fame essence and truly live your life through your fame character, you can move on to the next step: knowing your superfan.

Tension starts with your superfan, just like when you begin any new relationship and start to understand the difference between you and your partner to learn a new language of communication. The differences between you provide an opportunity to develop new habits, to create a new world of ideas.

How do we use this tension strategically and thoughtfully in marketing ourselves? Do you know your superfan? What is unique about your brand? How is it different? Can you define your brand essence? Building tension, and finding your superfan, is easy, but you need to do it consciously and with a method that holds to the brand.

Apple, the Master of Tension-Building

Why does Apple keep leading and growing while others follow and copy?

Because Apple has a clearly defined brand character, and they know how to create powerful chemistry by building tension with its superfan.

When we build a brand from scratch, the brand needs a personality and personal values to represent what the founder believes in. Developing all this usually happens unconsciously. If the company culture is strong enough, it will withstand any storm. If not, it will slowly die. Now, if the brand is an accumulation of individuals and they don't define it well, and it stands for nothing, then before it expands, it will fail to attract a superfan and slowly dissolve.

Therefore, we like Apple because this tension is palpable in that company, and we want that energy in our lives. We've already said that Apple behaves like an Outlaw and continues to disrupt and revolutionize every industry it touches. So why is an Outlaw brand making a gallery of beautiful artwork? Simple. Because the opposite of the Outlaw is the Creator, and the Creator makes beautiful and innovative artwork.

Because the company's fame essence strategically communicates in a way that attracts their opposite. Companies that connect to the heart and soul of their audience naturally do this. Apple's Creators Gallery posts and promotes beautiful, disruptive crafters' work. Rather than being overly disruptive, Apple focuses on celebrating others' works and creativity in their gallery.

Apple does this intuitively so well. They give their superfans a platform to showcase themselves and play with Apple tools on Instagram. Apple's fame character is the Outlaw (breaks convention, revolutionizes), and their opposite is the Creator (perfectionist, precision). Instead of using Outlaw language, Apple builds tension by adding actions that appeal to the Creator.

Let's look at two other great brands: Starbucks and Coca-Cola.

As we've established, Starbucks behaves in the world as an Explorer. So why is an Explorer enticing you with luscious treats? For example, Starbucks' posts promote tasty products and experiences that tease a Lover's nature into daily delight! The opposite of the Explorer is the Lover, so rather than overemphasizing the Explorer, they focus on enjoying everyday experiences and indulging in tasty treats, reflecting the Lover's traits.

As noted before, Coca-Cola behaves in the world as an Innocent. So, why is an Innocent provoking conversation with relatable messages to unite people? Because the opposite of the Innocent is the Good Guy/Girl Next Door. Rather than overly communicating Innocent ideals, Coca-Cola strives to be inviting and relatable to all. Because their superfan is the Good Guy/Girl Next Door, we see more images of people coming together for joyous gatherings.

Tension Is a Beautiful Thing

Tension is a beautiful thing and should not be ignored; it is one of the most significant ways to cultivate and catapult your customer relationships forward. It is essential to be aware of the tension between you and your customer, to play on it, and not to ignore it. Know when intense tension will arise and acknowledge its existence so you remember where your superfan is coming from. Tension is built when we stretch our brand toward its opposite, which is how we create its differentiation in the marketplace.

Building tension is the secret sauce to sustaining clients. All your clients will not be your perfect client, but when you speak and act out of the right fame character and develop your superfan, you will set the bar so that when a client who is not optimal approaches you, you can say you are not interested in taking them on. Then again, why not keep them around if they want to stay?

Questions to Ponder:
- *Take your fame character and write five values that define your personal brand.*
- *Take your superfan and write five values that define them.*
- *Write five ways you can add tension to your brand.*
- *Write five things that differentiate you from your competitors based on your fame character.*
- *Write five things your superfan loves.*
- *Write five messaging strategies based on how you defined your fame character and superfan.*

Step 4: Know Your Path

Branding is the art of differentiation.
—David Brier

What Is the Customer Journey?

The customer journey begins with different phases where you surprise and delight your customer, creating the ultimate brand loyalty, retention, and referral program. Defining the journey lays the path to success, and in this way, it differentiates you from your competitors.

Brand differentiation helps you break through the clutter in the market. What is the look of your brand? What is your message? How are you different from your competitors?

Creating an Out-Of-The-Box Experience

What is an out-of-the-box experience? It refers to unpacking a box or product packaging. The out-of-the-box experience is a superfan's memorable interaction with you, your product, or your services. It is boxing you, the product, for the first time.

This act includes bespoke packaging and branded boxes, attractive details, and making it unforgettable.

Think of a time when you wanted to leave the store and go home, excited to unpack your purchase. All you wanted to do was open the box and start using your new products immediately. When you pulled the box lid, a surprising, beautiful detail emerged.

Here's another example. Let's say you are in the perfume section of a department store and see all the various options. All the perfume boxes are different—small and large—they feel like beautiful pieces of art. Select one perfume that resonates with you. The bottle feels solid, and a transparent liquid is placed exquisitely on the package. There is no need for an instruction manual. You take off the lid, remove the bottle, remove the cap, and push down on the spray pump. The fragrance top is the first thing you see. The simple package keeps the delicate bottle protected.

The leading role in the unboxing experience goes to the first thing you see: the fabulous bottle—unique, unexpected, and delightful. A thoughtful, out-of-the-box experience that creates a pleasant surprise for superfans and an experience never to forget.

Brand Experience Outcome:
    #1 Create Your Superfan Journey
    #2 Make Your Superfan Worth More
    #3 Measures to Success

Clients will transition through several phases as they use your product/service, each phase building on the previous. All these steps are uniquely defined by psychology. By deeply understanding your superfan, you design an experience that delights them.

Many consultants talk about the need to know your avatars—ideal clients, in the plural. Isn't it great to see that you only need one? And when someone asks who your superfan is, you can say it in three words and have the formula to reach them consistently. Your superfan is the person who picks you over price because your brand essence and story deliver on your unique map. Your success depends on how you connect with your superfan. How does your superfan perceive you and connect with you and your values?

Your business will be short-lived if you don't excite your superfan. The brand will only survive if you delight them time after time. How do you do this? Understanding their desires, what makes them frustrated, what keeps them up at night, and what they are proud of will give you the insight to develop the experience needed to accelerate your business.

Brand experiences are positive experiences that facilitate deeper connections, inspire the superfan, and ultimately deliver results. A positive brand experience can often mean the difference between being chosen repeatedly or losing the sale forever.

The challenge today is that the market is saturated with products and services, and the opportunity is to build a brand that breaks through the clutter and deeply resonates with your ideal client.

Your Purpose: Why?
"Why" you exist: The higher-order reason for being for a brand or business than just "making a profit or driving shareholder value."

Your Vision: Where?

"Where" you want to go: This is a destination, what you want your brand to be in the future (e.g., "We want to be the world's leader in xxx by 2020").

Your Mission: What?

"What" you should do to get there: These could be specific initiatives or tactics centered on product development, operational excellence, go-to-market strategies, or brand communications. "One purpose, many missions" is a phrase that brings it to life for me.

Your Core Values: How?

"How" you would like to behave to get there: What is the organizational culture of a company or an organization? And what are the qualities or behaviors it values? For instance, curiosity, inclusivity, diversity of thought, and so on.

Putting It All Together

Brands suggest factors that compel us to buy a particular product. First, we are instantly drawn to a specific brand. We are drawn to powerful brands because of their values, and they reflect what we want or want to become. Brands that trigger buying impulses do so because of the emotional factor built into them.

Brands have the power to drive behavior on an instinctive and subconscious level. Like a fragrance, they possess strong associative properties that quickly alter the mood, promoting increased alertness and positivity or creating feelings of calm, tranquility, and relaxation. They can help ease stress and insomnia and provide clarity and focus, and so can the power of brands.

Brands are like magic. Once you form the concept of a brand, it will transform you and others. Brands can drive impact and create the life of your dreams, and they will also challenge you to do things that may stop you in your tracks. Are you ready to make your dreams come true? Magic can be scary, but it also can be fun, and most of all, it can invigorate the senses and make the impossible possible.

Knowing your brand inside and out can bring power to who you are. This undeniable attraction you exude—just like when wearing your signature fragrance—attracts people toward you and wisely uses your power.

Mission: How would you describe your mission as an outfit if asked? Mine is a short Steve McQueen black full-feathered skirt with a small tail on the back. Wearing your mission transports us back to a specific memory or place; it creates a safe space for us to reminisce and escape into our imagination. Since our mission is one of the leading identity components, it's like an identification tag that gives us individuality.

The mission statement that defines a brand is the aim for us to reach our goals in life. A mission statement describes the desired future position of our brand. The clearer our mission, the more we can build energy and strive for purpose, creating goals and values.

What does a mission statement look like? Mission: To attract and attain superfans with high-value products and services and the most satisfying experience in the world. My mission is to be the world's most successful and respected brand strategist. The vision lies within the mission, where they clarify how they "inspire the world" and "create the future."

Coco Chanel's mission was to reinvent fashion by transcending its conventions, creating an uncomplicated luxury that would change women's lives forever.

Vision: Visions are like dreams. They are powerful and can enhance moods and change behavior! Visions can alter moods because they encourage the release of endorphins, just like a fragrance, making us feel good about our actions.

Visions give us a clear sense of purpose. It means we have a much bigger picture of our brand or life than simply setting and reaching short-term goals and tackling problems as they come along.

Visions let us dream. Dreaming is part of creating the unexpected, the unstoppable, the unforgettable goal we have for ourselves. What is that for you? Remember, anything is possible. Feel it, see it, sense it.

Coco Chanel envisioned a world where women had the power and status to make anything possible.

Purpose: Your brand purpose is your why. It is the reason your brand exists, the meaning behind your brand, and a view of what you want to become in the eyes of your superfan. Your brand purpose adds value to your audience and society as a whole. Having a brand purpose can help you build a more emotional relationship between your brand and its superfan, which helps boost sales and loyalty. A unique brand purpose can differentiate your brand from your competition.

To know your brand purpose, ask yourself: What does your brand stand for? What does your brand believe?

Coco Chanel's purpose was to create timeless designs, trademark suits, and little black dresses. In the 1920s, she launched Chanel No. 5 and introduced the Chanel suit and the little black dress, emphasizing making clothes more comfortable for women and liberating them from corsets.

Values: Values are the notes of a fragrance. Notes are divided into top/head notes, middle/heart notes, and base notes, denoting scents that can be sensed after applying the fragrance.

You are formulating your brand personality by defining its notes, and brand personality is one of the essential elements in driving recognition.

Your brand's values are the heart and soul of what your company does. They help you frame your creation story in a way that resonates with your superfan. Values matter because they serve as a reminder that behind every brand or business is a human being—give your brand a human face.

Brand values determine your brand's identity, message, and personality. These brand principles guide your creation story, actions, behaviors, and your unique decision-making processes.

Investing the time in knowing your brand values is fundamental to ensuring your business remains unique in a saturated market.

Brand values are guiding principles that shape every aspect of your business. They're placed at the very foundation of your brand and dictate your brand message, identity, and personality. For example, Coco Chanel's values were to follow no rules, epitomizing the modern values of freedom, passion, and feminine elegance.

Your Story: A brand isn't just something you create thoughtlessly; it's an extension of your feelings and experiences.

A creation story is a purpose behind what you stand for. If you don't have a story, you're missing something vital, an emotional hidden secret everyone wants to know.

You're missing your chance to stand out and the opportunity to form a lasting connection with others. But, most importantly, you're losing the relationship needed to connect with your superfan during the discovery phase.

Your creation story can be more than the history behind your brand and more intricate than a mission statement you wrote up in a meeting—although both can shape the story you want people to know.

Reach for the stars. Your brand creation story can encompass the feelings and facts behind your brand. It's a story, after all. Stories cause readers to feel emotions, and you can influence how your superfan's emotions can connect with you and your story.

It's not just words either; just like a fragrance, the notes and the shape of the bottle will affect your superfans emotionally, too.

Story Example (Chanel No. 5): In the 1920s, Coco Chanel launched Chanel No. 5. It remains an iconic fragrance to this day.

Coco Chanel had an idea for a fragrance but needed more expertise. She asked Ernest Beaux, one of the best perfumers of his time, to create the fragrance's formula. He had five samples to show her—and the last one, the fifth one, earned a place in Coco Chanel's heart.

Her favorite number was five. The perfume launched on the fifth day of the fifth month (May 5), and there were five essential notes in the fragrance.

This story proves that Coco Chanel knew her brand and purpose in creating the iconic Chanel No. 5. The name connects to her life. It's memorable and provides the connection people need, such as a fabulous, powerful businesswoman behind one of the world's most famous fragrances. The stars were aligned perfectly around her lucky number (remember, a star has five points).

Questions to Ponder:
Look at yourself as a fragrance:
- *How do you look? How do you want to be perceived?*
- *What personality do you have, i.e., smell? (Look at your fame character for guidance.)*
- *What makes you unique from the rest?*
- *How are you different from your competitors? How are your features and benefits different? What is the same? What do your customers or clients like about you, your products, or your services?*

Step 5: Know Your Destination

The way to get started is to quit talking and begin doing.
—Walt Disney

The five steps to fame are about getting clear about your destination. Do you envision the end? Have you planned for what's coming next in your business? Are you ready to take the stage? Then take it and make it real.

Getting Ready for the Show
What does it mean to launch? A launch is an act of putting something in motion. Launching

takes planning, resources, a guest list, the channels you plan to advertise, your team, and the tiny details, such as program, tickets, PowerPoint, announcer, strategy, and much more.

Having led several events, including Louisville Bespoke, here is my thought process for organizing an event using Chanel as an example. This is to give you an idea of what it will take to create a campaign to build your fame brand.

Select a Date

The date of your event is one of the most important elements. The date is everything. Chanel launched her fragrance on May 5. Five was her lucky number. You can pick any date, but if it's in person, you must look at all the events that day. Knowing the date eight months before launch will give you time to connect the dots, and people can save the date.

Theme

Having a theme for your event or launch will make your life easy. Do you have a unifying theme that your superfan has? Create a theme and make yourself more memorable. Embrace the theme and cascade your entire event from that unifying theme.

A unifying theme is the one word/thought driving your event/book/product/course. It's much like you'd have at a theme wedding or party, and everyone conforms to the theme. In the same way, an event should have a single theme running right through, which then binds everything together.

The theme will make your event memorable; your team will be able to come up with ideas, and your superfan will remember it—just like your fragrance.

For example, let's take a look at the Triumph of Bacchus as a fragrance. Bacchus was considered the god of winemaking, fertility, ritual madness, theater, and religious ecstasy. He was one of the twelve Olympians, although he was the last to arrive. He was often called Eleutherius, meaning "the liberator," because his wine, music, and ecstatic dance freed mortals from self-consciousness and the restraints of society. Bacchus crossed the boundary between life and death, between the known and unknown. He was a god of chaos and a protector of misfits. This luxurious scent is shrouded in grandeur and mystery.

Wildly romantic and fragrant notes dance beautifully together in harmony. Argos's Triumph of Bacchus is an exotic fragrance opening with spicy saffron, royal green apple, and rhum notes. Confident and refined tobacco is paired perfectly with amber and vanilla, revealing a powerfully seductive, almost sinful aphrodisiac. The theme for the event could represent the God Bacchus. You could make the entire experience about Roman times, connecting music, rituals, and luxury with the event.

There could be a wine-tasting area. The fragrance could be sprayed to bring in the notes and connect the scent with the product. Make the tickets for the event reflect the graphics of Roman times. We are using all the senses to relate to every detail.

Plan

What's the plan? You have everything you stand for, so what's the plan? Set priorities, focus energy and resources, strengthen operations, ensure that your team and the other stakeholders work toward common goals, establish agreement around intended outcomes/results, and assess and adjust the business goal.

What's the plan of attack? Do you have a goal? What's your monetary goal? Viewing it from the perspective of going to battle is essential, and you are here to win.

> *If you know the enemy and know yourself, you need not fear the result of a hundred battles. If you know yourself but not the enemy, for every victory gained, you will also suffer a defeat. If you know neither the enemy nor yourself, you will succumb in every battle.*
> —**Sun Tzu,** *The Art of War*

Look at your enemy as your competition. Do you know who they are? Do you know their strategies? What do they do best? If so, you are off to a great start. Remember what your brand stands for, remember your superfan, and take one step at a time toward the finish line.

Team

The best launches have the best teams. The team will get you through the good times and the bad. Who do you need on your team? What are each of their responsibilities, and why? How will you reward this fantastic team?

The team needs to be diverse. Each person should have a role and a task. The team should be small. Too many people can add optional complexity. Have one person make all final decisions. The smaller groups report directly to the person in charge. That person does not need to be the boss, and it's better if they are not.

The team should have an unrelated or similar task, and you have two groups executing the same thing. A great team can function, come together, and manage direction quickly and assertively. Think of it as giving different fragrance notes to the team and having them get each one correct, coming together at the end as one fragrance.

Guest List

To shape your event, you need to think strategically. Who do you want to invite as your VIP? Who can bring influence to the table? How can you connect the theme to the famous guests? The invitations you make are what's necessary to succeed.

Guests are like the ingredients of the fragrance. Each one has a purpose, and each one comes and goes. The complexity of the notes brings intrigue and makes them more desirable.

Channels

Distribution channels are essential to businesses as they allow for the smooth delivery of goods or services to a superfan. Channels create utility, improve exchange, and help match supply and demand. Each channel has a different potential for making sales.

An advertising channel is a medium a company uses to advertise its products and inform the superfan about promotions. As a result, television, radio, and print advertising are now used to connect technology-based advertising, like e-mails, websites, blogs, and so on.

What are the changes that benefit your event the most? No need to go for all the channels available. Select three or four and go full speed ahead.

Channels are like putting together a formula. Just because you have resources, it doesn't mean you need to use all the ingredients. Select the top five elements that will give you the sophistication to drive success.

Publicist

A publicist is a person whose job is to generate and manage publicity for a company, a brand, a public figure, or a work, such as a book, an event, or a movie.

A publicist helps you craft and tell your story to your audience in a compelling, relatable, and unique way. They ensure minute details are never missed and that your brand is packaged and presented in a way that helps you and your brand tell your best story.

A publicist's responsibility is to ensure that your brand is always portrayed positively in the public eye. Duties include managing day-to-day media relations, as well as the social media accounts of your brand.

They say the devil is in the details. Take everything from programs to seating charts, tickets, posters, flowers, placements, food, and everything else, and think through each detail.

Make sure your team takes the theme to heart and executes the details with it in mind. The music, the lighting, the gifts—EVERYTHING!

If Coco Chanel hadn't looked at the bottle's details and the dates she had selected to launch, I wonder if she would have been so successful. The details are the execution, and the execution matters.

The Story

What is the story you want people to know about you? Coco Chanel created her story because she wanted people to know about her. Create your power story and stand up for your beliefs.

What Is the Fragrance You Want to Leave Behind?

Branding is essential because it leaves a memorable impression on your superfan and allows them to know what to expect from your brand. It is a way of distinguishing yourself from your competitors and clarifying what you stand for and what makes you the better choice. Your brand is built to represent who you are as a business and how you wish to be perceived.

Leave behind the fragrance of success and the legacy you want to be known for.

Chapter 30

Overcoming the Barriers to Fame

There are no constraints on the human mind, no walls around the human spirit, no barriers to our progress except those we ourselves erect.
—Ronald Reagan, former U.S. President

Embracing the Magic of Fame
The world has changed, and we need to embrace it. Are you ready to take on the world? Your answer:

"Yes, I am. I want to be at the top and be number one, and I deserve it."

Being recognized for what you do is about overcoming naysayers, limiting beliefs, and yourself. You are your own most significant barrier to becoming famous.

We all hear that fame changes people suddenly, and research shows that fame can change a person's life forever, and it sometimes seems more like a shocking, "overnight" experience rather than a gradual transition. And that can make us fear it.

There is a logical explanation for why it affects us that way. We don't take the time to understand our true fame essence. But when we do, and we break away from all the other barriers we self-inflict, we can succeed and be happy in our fame.

Some of these barriers include the following:

I'm Not Getting Clients
Why are you not making sales? It could be a slew of factors.
   – *Are you selling the right product or service?*

- *Are you selling to your superfan?*
- *Do you portray your true essence to the world?*
- *Are you completely confident in yourself and your capability?*

You are the brand, whether you know it or not. You are the product, and it all hinges on belief in yourself. If you are confident in your authentic self, you can sell anything, and no one will say no.

For the longest time in my business, I was not making sales. I was giving away my services for free because I didn't believe in the product or myself. I started to see my clients succeed, which gave me the confidence to sell more, double my price, and even be okay with letting clients go. Sales are all about psychology and understanding human behavior, but there was a time when I could not do it, even with all the theories in my head. It's all about being ready to shed the false identity you have been holding on to. Shed the lies you tell yourself. Create a positive network, tell your story, and don't be afraid because anything is possible!

I'm Not Getting Invited

If you are waiting on the sidelines, you will not be invited. You have to take action. You have to spend money, and you have to connect. There are no ifs, ands, or buts about this part. You may not be invited because you are not doing what you strategically need to do.

- *Have you written out your big, audacious goal? One that excites and energizes you?*
- *Do you know where you want to go?*
- *If the answer is no, what are you waiting for?*

Write down your dream, find your people, and tell your story. Go out there and be you. When I started my fashion business, I was not getting invited places. So, I reached out to people I already knew. I met for coffee or tea. I called people out of the blue. I would tell my story and the vision I had for the community. That simple act of connecting with others in the community grew my business exponentially. I had coffee and lunch with two people a day for two months. That was the best strategy I could have taken. I got invited to everything and found another way in when I didn't. Pursue your dream with courage and do whatever it takes because it will open doors you never thought possible.

I'm Not Growing
The cost of not being famous is high, and you may feel stuck.
- *Why isn't my business growing?*
- *Did I choose the wrong career?*
- *Is there more out there for me?*
- *Why am I not making money?*
- *Why is this so hard?*

There are so many unanswered questions about not moving and not growing. I looked for answers outside of me. I would set up calls with psychics, numerologists, astrologers, and crystal healers. (I love all that woo-woo stuff.) It would always reveal the same answer. I had to look within and ask myself a few simple questions:
- *What was I looking for in my life?*
- *What did I want?*
- *What was the one thing I needed to do to move my business forward? It can be paralyzing and super-easy to do nothing and avoid the task ahead.*

The first question to ask yourself is, "Are you ready?" Will you do whatever it takes? If the answer is yes, there is nothing that can stop you!

I was working on my business, and this was the second time around after a failed attempt the year before. I was selling, but I needed more.

I asked myself often, "Should I get a 'real' job?"

I loved my life. I loved helping women understand the possibilities of their businesses and create the work of their dreams. I loved what I was doing. I didn't want to go back to a nine-to-five and work on someone else's dream. I wanted to work on my dream and work over forty hours a week plus weekends because I was in my element and creating magic.

I'm Not Being Recognized
Not being recognized can stem from many things. When we are not being recognized, the question is usually: Am I working in my fame zone?

There is a strategy for getting recognized. Putting ourselves out there is sometimes the most challenging thing. If we don't put ourselves out there, nothing will happen. You will be the best-kept secret in town. When fear rears its head, we need to recognize, acknowledge, and take tiny steps toward it. There was a time in my life when I was doing so much and felt like everything I did was in vain. But being recognized does not depend on the time you've spent pursuing it. It depends on how badly you want it and if you are willing to do what it takes.

Are you willing to start at zero?

If you are too tired, too busy, and too stressed by other things, don't bother. Part of taking the path to fame is recognizing where to put your energy. Yes, I'm sure you have unique ideas and dreams, but you need to focus on the one thing you are going after and put all your energy into that.

We put energy into a hundred things, and it gets dispersed, which is why things take longer. I know. For many years, I did it. I was playing with four different businesses, and in my head, I thought, *The more I do, the easier it will be to find the one that sticks*. It doesn't work that way.

How many businesses are losing out because they are not focusing on building relationships and being the thought leaders in their space? The cost is high for those who haven't focused on fame. Think about what has been happening during the pandemic. Many companies have not factored the fame factor into withstanding the crisis. Showing the world you still exist, even in a crisis or lockdown, and having the knowledge and expertise to move forward into the future is the key to long-lasting success.

> *I always say to people that if they want to achieve the level of notoriety that I've achieved, it requires doing 10,000 small steps.*
> —**David Meerman Scott, author and marketing strategist**

Chapter 31

Advice and Other Thoughts on Fame from the Pros

After working with a client who has gone on to conquer their industry, we love to check in and ask them to tell us about the moment they knew they had become famous. That moment is always a little surprising and magical, and for us, it's an absolute joy and honor to hear their feedback and perspective. We want to share a few of these stories with you.

The Life Coach

I know I did not start this business to become famous; fame was not an incentive for me. I just wanted to do great. Deep work impacts people, especially women, to become the best version of themselves. Initially, I was thrilled to sit in my little office, talk to my clients by phone, and hide out and not go out in the world, but I think fame is an exciting question because I've now seen its significant importance and joy.

But when did I know? I was coaching a woman who owned a magazine. She hired me to coach her because she was freaking out, like what did I take on? What did I do? We started working together, and she could not afford to pay me, but she could give me advertising in her magazine. I never thought anyone would hire a coach through advertising, but her designer was the graphic designer of my brand. So, there was this lovely connection, and my designer understood how to create the ads that reflected my brand. Every month they changed the advertisement according to the magazine's theme. Then, a few months into coaching her, she invited me to write a column for the magazine. I also ran ads next to the column, which I designed, so it felt really on brand. The column wasn't just talking *at* people; I involved them. I brought them in. I included coaching questions. I added a helpful list.

After several months of doing this, I was in a Starbucks, and this woman came to me and asked, "You're the woman who writes that column in the magazine, aren't you?"

I said, "Yes, I am," not sure what was coming next.

She said, "I want to thank you. I have kept every single column. I cut them out. I put them on my refrigerator and do every exercise, and you have changed my life so much."

Wow! Writing this column made me famous in a new community. I had already been in a prominent community role. I was the president of the Junior League in Louisville, so I had these same community-based roles. This put me on the map as an inspiring person with wisdom. To this day, when I meet people who say, "I know you from somewhere," it still is often from that magazine column.

That was when I said to myself, "You're starting to make some impact. People are listening to what you say. You are having a positive influence on people, which is what you wanted to do!"

> *I've always been a person that really didn't dive too headfirst into wanting and needing attention. I mean, we all love attention, but for me, I don't necessarily adore it. I use it when I want to communicate something.*
> —**Rapper Kendrick Lamar,** *Citizen Magazine*

The Beauty Entrepreneur

Everyone has their own idea of what that means, but the first time I remember being recognized outside of my social circle, I was at the airport at about seven o'clock in the morning.

I was just getting coffee, and this woman approached me and said, "I know you don't know me, but I'm one of your customers. I love your products so much, and I just saw you, and I just had to come and say thank you so much for making such great products." It almost took my breath away because I hadn't been on the *Today* show. I hadn't been on QVC yet. At that time, my exposure was nothing like later on. The other people in the coffee line started to take notice, too: "Who are you? Is she somebody we should know?"

I don't know if I would call it fame, but that is when I realized I had become a public figure, at least in a small way, and that I would only continue to grow.

The truth is, I only really knew I'd made it once the female impersonators started doing me in their acts.
—Bette Davis, as portrayed by Susan Sarandon in the TV series Feud

The Ph.D. Extraordinaire

I realized I was known in my own city when I walked into cafes and people recognized me. And the sad thing is, I didn't think I was famous back then. I thought I was infamous. I came to this city, and I instigated a lot of change at this art college, and I did it really fast, which nobody was used to, and I think I was like a firestorm for these poor people. They were extremely mad at me, and the local newspapers followed every move I made. At the same time, some of the city was celebrating me. Some people called me one of the most influential people in town, while others were just keeping a close eye on me, like, "Guess what she's doing now?"

And so I was in the papers, and it was shocking for me because I'm a quiet person. It was terrible and interesting. But I realized that there is no such thing as bad press. You know, the minute you become a topic that people are interested in hearing about, that can only be good for your organization, so I aim to be as infamous as possible and as troublesome as I can so that we can move forward.

I want to poke holes in the erroneous beliefs about what fame provides. It won't raise your self-esteem, it won't create profound connection, it's not going to heal your childhood traumas.
—Alanis Morissette

The Consultant

I think it was a couple of years ago my daughter came to me and said, "Hey, Mom, you're Google-able!"

I'm blessed to have had a couple of public-facing visible roles that required me to demonstrate a level of conspicuousness and articulate points of view with fair regularity. When I realized what I espouse, who I am, and the work that I do transcend my local community and are getting out into the ether, that was probably when I knew.

The Brand Photographer

There was one moment when I looked at myself in the mirror and said, "Girl, you've got it going on." It's seeing yourself in that role. I had gone through a lot of behind-the-scenes deep-diving work on my writing. In working on courses, I had worked deeply on the authenticity piece coming from the inside out. I started showing up online in podcast interviews more *myself* than I had been in a very long time. And when that happened, the invitations started flowing in, the referrals started flowing in, and even more cool was that I started getting these behind-the-scenes messages from other photographers, creatives, and business owners saying things like, "Jama, I love everything you're doing. Can you show me how you're doing that? It can't be easy." When people felt compelled to reach out to me, I realized, well, we can call it fame, or we can just call it somebody seeing you for the first time, but that's when all that happened, and it was beautiful.

The woman who can create her own job is the woman who will win fame and fortune.
—*Amelia Earhart*

The Healer

It's interesting how the word *fame* brings up a lot of emotion. I would say that being invited to events by people I don't know, like friends of friends or people sharing a lot of my business through referrals. When people I've served shared their experiences and I started to hear from many new people, none of whom I have ever met, it was a monumental moment for me. My presence, energy, and calling are being radiated out into the universe, and now I'm getting to expand on that. That would be my defining moment.

Fame is a four-letter word, and like tape or zoom or face or pain or life or love, what ultimately matters is what we do with it.
—*Fred Rogers*

The Business Developer

Fame can look very different to different people, so what comes to mind happened kind of recently. I was honored to be recognized as a 40 Under 40 leader last year, and, of course, I was going to lean into my brand. The organization asked me if I would feature a talent that I have, and I agreed. I love salsa dancing and all the Latin dances, so I decided to record myself dancing with my son Isaiah on my shoulders to one of my favorite salsa songs. It turned out to be a hit. People loved the video. They showed it at the awards event, and when it was time for me to go up and receive my award, I wanted to harken back to my brand, so I decided I had to dance right on stage after I got my award. Now when I meet people around town, they ask, "Why do I know you?" And then I see it click for them, and they'll say, "Hey! You're that guy who salsa danced on stage at the 40 Under 40!"

The light of the dawn is not so sweet as the first glimpses of fame.
—Luc de Clapiers

The MD Superwoman

It was probably four or five years ago when I attended a play with my husband. These women walked up to me and asked, "Are you Dr. Ariana?" I said yes, and they got very excited and began saying, "Oh, we just love you! We follow you!" They caught me off guard since I was out for the weekend, and it was so out of context. It dawned on me that had to be how celebrities feel sometimes. People just walk up and start talking to you. So, it was a little off-putting for me because when they first asked me who I was, I wondered if I should say yes or no. I didn't know if they would say something nice or not. Luckily, they were very positive. It just dawned on me that, *Wow, you know.* I was doing a lot of ads in one of the local magazines, and my face was being seen a lot and the city I live in is not huge. Being recognized took some getting used to, even when people were saying nice things.

Fame for fame's sake is a completely empty experience. Fame should be a by-product (and not necessarily a good one) of achieving something extraordinary.
—Rita Rudner

—————— Conclusion:

From Every Ending Comes A New Beginning

Never be afraid to stop traffic.
—Iris Apfel

Everyone has a gift in this world. If your gift is to serve your clients with your expertise, your fame will be honorable, as will what we do for our clients. You don't want to be the best-kept secret for people not to receive the immense value you bring to this planet.

So many of us stay small because it's comfortable. We think: *I'm not good enough. Who needs this, anyway? Why do all this, and for what?*

But for some of us, it's something we can't control. Something inside us won't let us stop, and we push through the difficulties, the hard times, and the critics.

We know we are meant for more, and we keep moving forward, not knowing what's ahead but the feeling of accomplishing what we set out to do.

Fear numbs us and doesn't let us fulfill our dreams and desires. You will feel like something is missing in your life.

Be courageous like Iris Apfel and put yourself out there like no one is watching. Ask for help and continue the path to fame.

Fame is just a four-letter word. Find your definition of pursuing your greatness, whatever that is for you.

Know yourself, your values, your purpose, and your vision just by knowing that you will accomplish more than you've ever imagined.

Imagine, be curious, and take action!

When I look back at my life, there is much to be thankful for. I grew up in a family of six; I was the oldest, and I was the boss. I was strong-willed and intelligent, and I led my siblings into my creative world.

My childhood was happy, moving from country to country and taking in all life experiences. Good grades were important to me, and taking on challenges was my bread and butter.

Not much changed in my teenage years. Grades were still important. I was still a traveler, and my creative world opened up. The one thing that changed was that I had to get creative with how I led because now I was no longer the tallest in the room.

I rebelled late in my life. In my twenties, I left my comfortable home and ran away with a boy. That experience ended in divorce. I left my country and moved to the U.S. alone. I had always wanted to study in the U.S., and I made it happen, not without difficulties. I made what I thought was impossible possible.

From then on, I knew I could do things others were afraid to do. I had the capacity for more risk and the vision to see the future for myself and the projects and products I designed.

Now, I'm here, at this juncture, writing this book, living this life.

This is a new chapter for me, and this won't be my last book. Many more to come, more concepts to help guide the magic in you. This is just the beginning of a new page in the book of life.

The root is in the soul of existence. No matter can change the purpose of existence. It's more about discovering the soul of existence than the matter it contains.
—Dana Skrodzki

— Acknowledgments

To my husband, who has supported all my endeavors. I could not have realized my dreams without his love and support.

My mother has always believed in me and has encouraged me for as long as I can remember. Even when I made mistakes, she saw them as part of the journey to success.

My father, who saw the real me and let me be me and at times guided me back to what I was meant to be.

To Sabrina, who guided, mentored, and helped me find the path to understanding branding from the perspective of psychology and the power of archetypes. Her laugh when things got super-exciting and her drive to do extraordinary things.

Torund encouraged me to write and told me I could write because I never thought I was good at writing. For the concepts we created, the work we did together, the travels, and the friends she shared with me.

To Jennifer Blair, my bestie. She has listened and guided me through hard times and good times. She has been such a fantastic friend and confidante.

To my clients, every single one of them who has believed in my work and the possibility of their brand.

To Betty Hines, my mentor. Betty has been my guiding light and the support every woman of color needs to scale and grow their business. Thank you to the WEW team of incredible women.

To Jeannette, my dear friend, who tells it how it is. She's always there for me and is full of knowledge and wisdom.

Carol S. Pearson, author of *Awakening the Heroes Within* and *The Hero and the Outlaw*. The books inspired my theories and unlocked the possibility maker in me.

Tam Luc for giving me the confidence to take my business into the stratosphere and for supporting my business and method.

Jodi Vetterl for believing in me, encouraging me, and bringing me my first clients.

Didi Wong, my mentor. She has taken me to places I would have never imagined going.

Nura, my walking confidante. She has guided me along the way with her wise words and knowledge.

Elizabeth Olson, my mentor, and together we discuss all subjects. She is a wealth of knowledge.

Claudia has been a fantastic friend and confidante on this journey.

Stephanie, who guided me through the most remarkable healing journey.

There are so many individuals that have made an impact on my life. I'm grateful to all my teachers and people in every place I worked and the city of Louisville for receiving me with open arms.

Our Services

Bespoke Branding
Tailored Branding to Reach Your Ideal Client
Gain a deeper level of understanding to empower your
brand and purpose and rule the market.

– *Personal Branding*
– *Brand Identity*
– *Brand Strategy*
– *Brand Positioning*
– *Brand Consulting*
– *Brand Workshops*

References

Arons, Marc de Swaan. "How Brands Were Born: A Brief History of Modern Marketing." The Atlantic, October 3, 2011. Accessed January 11, 2023. https://www.theatlantic.com/business/archive/2011/10/how-brands-were-born-a-brief-history-of-modern-marketing/246012.

Brand Builders Group. "Trends in Personal Branding," n.d. Accessed January 11, 2023. https://brandbuildersgroup.com/study/.

Carufel, Richard. "Trends in Personal Branding: When Brand Aligns with Values, Most Americans Will Spend More." Agility PR Solutions, January 12, 2022. Accessed January 11, 2023. https://www.agilitypr.com/pr-news/public-relations/trends-in-personal-branding-when-brand-aligns-with-values-most-americans-will-spend-more/.

Encyclopedia Britannica. "Collective Unconscious," n.d. Accessed January 11, 2023. https://www.britannica.com/science/collective-unconscious.

Grand View Research. "Personal Development Market Size Report, 2020-2027." Accessed January 11, 2023. https://www.grandviewresearch.com/industry-analysis/personal-development-market.

Hall, Nancy. "Newton's Laws of Motion." Glenn Research Center. NASA, October 27, 2022. Accessed January 11, 2023. https://www1.grc.nasa.gov/beginners-guide-to-aeronautics/newtons-laws-of-motion/.

Haviland, Lou. "Lucille Ball and Vivian Vance's Friendship Was Tested during This Worst Moment on 'I Love Lucy.'" Showbiz Cheat Sheet, September 22, 2020. Accessed January 11, 2023. https://www.cheatsheet.com/entertainment/

lucille-ball-and-vivian-vances-friendship-was-tested-during-this-worst-moment-on-i-love-lucy.html/.

Holland, Taylor. "What Is Branding? A Brief History." Skyword, August 11, 2017. Accessed January 11, 2023. https://www.skyword.com/contentstandard/branding-brief-history/.

Jacobson, Sheri. "The Collective Unconscious - What Is It, and Why Should You Care?" Harley Therapy™ Blog, May 11, 2017. Accessed January 11, 2023. https://www.harleytherapy.co.uk/counselling/what-is-the-collective-unconscious.htm.

Joonko. "You Can't Prevent Unconscious Bias from Happening, so Stop Trying To." Medium, August 23, 2017. Accessed January 11, 2023. https://medium.com/@JoonkoHQ/you-cant-prevent-unconscious-bias-from-happening-so-stop-trying-to-3f7a7f20590e.

Mark, Margaret, and Carol Pearson. *The Hero and the Outlaw: Building Extraordinary Brands through the Power of Archetypes*. New York: McGraw-Hill, 2001.

McLeod, Saul. "Carl Jung's Theories: Archetypes, & the Collective Unconscious." Simply Psychology, May 21, 2018. Accessed January 11, 2023. https://www.simplypsychology.org/carl-jung.html.

Moorhead, Joanna. "Emma Thompson: 'Family Is about Connection.'" The Guardian, March 20, 2010. Accessed January 11, 2023. https://www.theguardian.com/lifeandstyle/2010/mar/20/emma-thompson-nanny-mcphee-2.

Oxford University Press. "Definition of 'Psychology Noun' from the Oxford Advanced Learner's Dictionary." Oxford Advanced Learner's Dictionary, 2019. Accessed January 11, 2023. https://www.oxfordlearnersdictionaries.com/definition/english/psychology.

The Guardian. "Facebook's Mobile Journey Has Only Just Begun, but Already Makes Money," February 3, 2014. Accessed January 11, 2023. https://www.theguardian.com/technology/2014/feb/03/facebook-mobile-desktop-pc-platforms.

Van Sickel, Elizabeth. "The Power of Story: How Understanding Our Narrative Transforms Our Perspective." Restored Hope Counseling Blog, December 14, 2017. Accessed January 11, 2023. https://www.restoredhopecounselingservices.com/blog/2017/12/14/the-power-of-story-how-understanding-our-narrative-transforms-our-perspective.

Printed in the United States
by Baker & Taylor Publisher Services